At Night On The Sun

At Night On The Sun

Will Alexander

chax
2017

Library of Congress Cataloging-in-Publication Data

Names: Alexander, Will, author.
Title: At night on the sun / by Will Alexander.
Description: First edition. | Victoria Texas : Chax Press, 2017.
Identifiers: LCCN 2017043874 | ISBN 9781946104090 (acid-free paper)
Classification: LCC PS3551.L357716 A95 2017 | DDC 812/.54--dc23
LC record available at https://lccn.loc.gov/2017043874

Chax Press / PO Box 162 / Victoria, TX 77902-0162

Chax Press is supported in part by the School of Arts & Sciences at the University
of Houston-Victoria. We are located in the UHV Center for the Arts in downtown
Victoria, Texas. We acknowledge the support of graduate and undergraduate
student interns and assistants who contribute to the books we publish. In Summer
2017 our interns are Julieta Woleslagle, Maria Edwards, and Renee Raven.
The book is also supported by private donors. We are thankful to all of our
contributors and members.

Please see http://chax.org/support/ for more information.

Contents

This enactment is certainly not imbued by literal fact, but ignited by imaginary zeal. It takes place shortly after Asoka's triumph over Kalinga. "Asoka had seen the bloodshed with his own eye and felt that he was cause of the destruction. The whole of Kalinga was plundered and destroyed. Asoka after seeing this was filled with sorrow and remorse." This play casts him in a liminal state evolving beyond a state of warfare towards a psychic plane not unlike that of Buddhism. Thus, an atmosphere is engaged that portrays a state of affairs suffused by a fraught liminality.

Characters

Asoka, Mauryan Emperor

Harappa, First Minister of War

Daro, Second Minister of War

Three Magicians

Four Women Mourners

Khonsu, Apparition

Pentaura, Egyptian Magician

Four Women Accusers

Chorus

Off Stage Voices

A Group of Soldiers

Place: Pataliputra capital of the Mauryan Empire

Time: Late 260 B.C.

ACT I

PHILOSOPHICAL BALLET

A pitch-dark room having an empty throne encircled by lighted candles. Within the encircling flame three magicians are circling the throne and chanting. The sound of thunder can be heard at scattered intervals punctuating the silence at scattered intervals, accompanied by lightning that irregularly illumines the chamber.

THE THREE MAGICIANS *(collectively chanting)*: He lives inside us as does botany and lightning. He is our solar halo, our advanced dictation, who ignites our thoughts with ferocious calm, with invisible seepage. He has ignited himself and crowned himself with the discipline of Saturn. Now we feed him moons so that he breathes, proving his aural with orchestras to transmute. Thus, he empowers our cryptic voice with puzzling inscrutables…

(As their sound trails away, the candles are suddenly extinguished. The stage goes dark, and the magicians, in their burnouse-like garb, disperse, becoming invisible in the dark. The stage is suddenly cast in dim, but normal lighting. The First and Second Ministers of War appear, Harappa and Daro. Harappa enters from stage left, and Daro, the Second Minister enters from stage right.)

HARAPPA *(concern in his voice)*: We regale the world with our power and the Emperor remains missing.

DARO *(matter-of-factly)*: He is to appear at The Table of the Ascendants.

HARAPPA: It seems he's fled to obscurity. Does he scatter his body amidst the reptiles? *(getting angrier)* Just give facts, when did he disappear? *(short pause)* Was he inebriated? What were the signs that appeared in the heavens?

DARO *(visibly bracing himself)*: You are my superior…

HARAPPA *(starting and stopping his pacing, then staring warily at Daro)*:
How am I to know these things since you tend to generally realize
yourself at the border of death. *(Louder)* What do the magicians know?

DARO: I've not consulted their findings.

HARAPPA *(more and more agitated)*: Then bring me aural dossiers, then
scribble notes from the fire of their verbal leakage.

DARO *(more firmly)*: You've humbled your own mind and made it part
of your wares.

HARAPPA: You're chiding me Daro, you're making…

DARO: Mockery. How can I make mockery when I have no seeming
power over you?

HARAPPA *(insistent)*: I've given you power. I've consulted your
thoughts when I've brooded over the empire.

DARO *(almost scornfully)*: So now you reap magic. You've revealed
the laws governing cyclical foundation. I'm assuming you've made
enemies fall dead without blows, and humbled vultures, and made
revenues accrue from the unfeasible.

HARAPPA *(pointing to himself)*: I was his first appointment.

DARO *(pointing back at him)*: You are the essence of an owl; Asoka
bickered with an owl in his sleep and chose you against his better
judgment.

HARAPPA *(moving threateningly forward)*: You're jealous. I've
maintained the revenues…

DARO (*without flinching*): Asoka wants to test our ordinary limits, to see if we're capable of rising from the dead.

HARAPPA: So you scheme with the magicians against me.

DARO: No, I know what I know from travels through sleep. I've been blessed with the powers of foresight.

HARAPPA (*in a less agitated tone*): How can you say this when our duties in life are scripted? We know that flowers rise, that grapes are weighed, that animals are slaughtered.

DARO: Every force encountered in life is not literal. The coffers, the children we conceive are extinct before they exist.

HARAPPA (*his hands trembling in anger*): So now you feel as if you were reading my mind. You're trying to make me struggle, you cast doubt inside my blood.

DARO: I've never scripted…

HARAPPA: Then give me your reasoning.

(*Pause*)

DARO (*calmly explaining*): Every night he goes missing and the magicians take over the chamber.

HARAPPA: You're implying that worldly power is lost at moonrise, that the magicians replace us, that all our calculation is for naught.

DARO: Everyday, the muscles lapse around my eyes. Day after day I've been forgetting myself, estranged from my own form. For this or that reason blankness engulfs me, the walls then blaze as opal and I seem to vanish from myself. *(Pause)* When we ignited flames in Kalinga, when Girika gouged eyes, and quartered skulls, Asoka never wavered, and was present every-nightfall. And now, since he considers his spoils to be vacant, he seems to vanish at moonrise.

HARAPPA: We need his guidance after our victory, we need his authorship of our conclave. *(Pause, very concerned)* If our unicity weakens, others may attack us, our heads may populate the pikes of our enemies. *(Nervously striding back and forth)* It's power...

DARO: The magicians want to tame us, they seek our well-being.

HARAPPA *(pointedly)*: What else do you know? Do they concoct vials from pure air? Do they make noises in your veins? Do they allow you to read the signs from blood on a scabbard?

DARO *(quietly)*: We're being tested.

HARAPPA *(suddenly animated)*: I've killed for Asoka, I've scripted dead bodies with my sword and drew comfort, I've rousted certain traitors and cooked them in tiger's venom.

DARO: Harappa the heavens have shifted, your birth star has exploded. It's obvious another direction has revealed itself.

HARAPPA: So I'm assuming Asoka has no birth star since he seems to have no fully scripted assignation. He is simply the Mauryan mind, the Mauryan soul.

DARO: Let me ask you, is there nothing but borders and the vertigo of bloodshed?

HARAPPA: What power do you aspire to? What type of pronouncement do you hold in your spirit?

Daro: You are consumed. You do nothing but harbor suspicion.

Harappa: Come now Daro we are always under suspicion. Some unsuspected enemy may surreptitiously consult a sorcerer and after three unsettled days I'll find vipers in my bedding, having, as consequence, a lack of oxygen in my blood.

Daro *(beginning to circle Harappa)*: You exaggerate and you simplify. You're mind courses through poison and ominously concurs with that poison. To you, I am the sigil who conspires, who reeks guilt and leaks blood. In this sense it is I who is not unlike the surreptitious sorcerer, who extracts an army of corpses from dazed wheat.

Harappa *(a forced calm in his voice)*: Let me see your ledgers.

Daro *(ceasing to circle Harappa)*: They are in order.

Harappa *(a derisive laugh)*: They're scrambled with blood. They have no contact with competence. *(pause)* Where is the land they represent?

Daro: You didactically project!

Harappa: Then why does Asoka strangely vanish and rise in the body at dawn?

Daro: You need ask him, you simply need ask him.

Harappa: I'm concerned for my neck, for what the Emperor has in store for me.

Daro: Is this why you continue to harangue me, and attempt to consume me with your unstable static?

HARAPPA: You're implying…

DARO: You know nothing but brutality, you could row a boat in soldier's blood.

HARAPPA: I know everything that must be gained or destroyed, I know the specific outlines of the general condition, I know when the coffers rise and fall, I know the roads, the flood plains, the weakness in the chains of command.

DARO: Yet Asoka can never gain trust when he continues to singe the populace by uttering fire as his basic pronouncement.

HARAPPA: Since I know the properties secured, the immolations we've had to conduct…

DARO: Has he ever spoken to you about his inner fire, about his treason against death?

HARAPPA: He knows I know about pressing affairs, about specific conditions as they arise.

DARO: Let me know Harappa, about the murders you've recently arranged?

HARAPPA (*shaking his head*): I refuse to pursue secrets.

DARO: Are you saying that there has never been a glossary of victims?

HARAPPA (*discomforted body language*): There exist no tallies that present themselves.

DARO: Of course you can't tell! I sense that you no longer respect Asoka in the absence of state-mandated violence. I sense that you sense that he does nothing other than grant favors to nothingness. To you, he hemorrages fever and is mentally feeble, with his hold over violence having vanished in thin air.

HARRAPA (muttering beneath his breath): You aspire to my position.

DARO: Speak clearly!

HARAPPA: You aspire to my position. I control the great forces!

DARO (sensing Harappa's non-stability): Then how do you account for Asoka and his spontaneous return via disappearance?

HARAPPA: So now I'm negated by the invisible, by the powers that absent the Sun from my grasp. (Pause) You cast Asoka in the abstract. (starting to walk in circles) What about the lands, the blood, the gain? Why do you stand here clothed and well fed? The reason, Daro, is death, you have lived and feasted off of death. It replicates and burns. It remains our master. This is what Asoka…

DARO (breaking in): You hold him in former alignment.

HARAPPA: Does not the emperor blaze because of blood that he's spilled? Does his legacy not soar because of the misery that he's authored?

DARO (shaking his head in disapproval): You're staging your own speech, you're making up your own importance. War is now a vanished claim. The concubines and corpses have now sunk into shadow.

HARAPPA (angered): You slander…

DARO: How can I slander when life has lifted itself to other regions?

HARAPPA: Sind has no threats? Do we protect ourselves with ghosts?

21

DARO: Dimensions have shifted.

HARAPPA: So this is now Asoka's dimension.
DARO: He's in transition.

HARAPPA (*sarcastically*): So now he tames lizards as his central distraction. So now he governs from the unseen as his throne is now in ascendance.

DARO: For you, it is always conflict, it is always an inferno of horses.

HARAPPA: I've sweltered, I've hunted danger, I've brought Asoka to the heights by means of my sword.

DARO (*a touch of bitterness*): He owes you nothing! You are only capable of the poverty of the visible.

HARAPPA (*beginning to circle Daro again with a threatening tone in his voice*): What else have you stamped on official tablature, perhaps argument for weakness and mercy, for loss of stamina in the blood? That I'm brewing political sorcery…

DARO (*breaking in once again*): You are extreme Harappa. You blunt the circumstance with your brazenness, yet you make up shadows and release them, all the while you have no evidence.

HARAPPA (*more excited*): You accuse me of sleeping with witches, of transposing my sperm with black eruptions from wheat.

DARO: I've never accused you of hissing through pus in your sleep, of fostering strangled motives, of tactically fomenting tactical inertia.

HARAPPA: You've admitted it. You side with Asoka in my downfall. (*Pause, emphatic*) Where is Asoka?

DARO: He self-ignites and inhabits the Sun during Sleep.

HARAPPA: He disappears just to plot against me, just to…

DARO: Nothing as such exists. You plot your own demise.

HARAPPA: Your point is clear. You emit the occult with your clarity. You've committed yourself to the ashen, to the unbelievable.

DARO: Everything for you evolves from visibility. For instance, numbers of hives, ledgers filled with ruined coinage.

HARAPPA: You abstract. Blood needs grow by living in soil.

(The two menacingly stare at one another from their respective angles.)

DARO: So blood for you is nothing more than owned property. Therefore peace can only amount to watch-full threat.

HARAPPA: This is how forces are crammed with power. This is how coffers overrun themselves with largesse.

(They imperceptibly move at greater distance from one another.)

DARO: Life has evolved…

HARAPPA: So that we can burn fires and build monuments to Asoka.

DARO: You're clinging to former mastery.

HARAPPA: So what is "former mastery"? My symbolic neutering? My death by un-goaded trance?

DARO: You scatter your birth chart with debris.

HARAPPA *(embittered)*: You cast personal aspersion. And you call yourself second in command. *(in a mocking tone)* You are emperor of negation. When Asoka returns he will accuse you of treason. How will you protect us against Aryans lurking at the edges of the land?

DARO: You boast Harappa, but I do nothing more than project fumes from the afterlife, from synonyms of sleep.

HARAPPA *(gesturing in muted triumph)*: You speak of sleep and I speak of blood.

DARO *(in sharp rejoinder)*: You revel in disunion. It allows your arrogance to burn.

HARAPPA *(getting angry again)*: I've tamed tigers…

DARO: I don't doubt your bravery or your stamina. Yet you've left nothing more than a sea of entrails.

HARAPPA *(boasting)*: I've left our enemies weakened. I've left them stammering with withdrawal.

DARO *(sternly)*: Command has shifted. You've failed at transmuting the blood thirst of your personal tenor.

HARAPPA: So now I constitute a race of brutes. So now, I am a forgone brute. I am fallen humanity.

DARO: Think as you wish.

HARAPPA: As I wish!

(Harappa begins moving closer to Daro as if to pull out his sword. Daro moves closer to Harappa doing the same. Thunder begins rumbling and lightning suddenly illumines the scene. A startled Harappa turns skyward.)

DARO: There are higher forces than the soils you seek to reconnoiter.

HARAPPA: You've rooted me in the despicable.

DARO *(calmly)*: Forces have transmuted.

HARAPPA *(barely containing himself)*: You conspire with Asoka against all that I have struggled for, against all the faith that Sind has placed in me, against all that Sind has understood as its greatness. *(Pause. Intermittent lightning)* You susurrate, you ruthlessly conspire.

DARO: Anger makes you slip and lose balance.

(The lightning ceases.)

HARAPPA: Into what am I slipping? All the vipers's nets you've cast about me, all the surgeries you seem to suggest.

DARO *(eyes cast upwards, his right arm pointed upward)*: The moon seems flooded with rain.

HARAPPA *(stridently)*: It's only dry dim light. So how can one chart crops, or plot one's destiny through its findings.

DARO: I feel contortion in your spirit. And because I feel it so strongly…

(Harappa begins to unsheathe his sword. Daro grips his arm. The two

struggle. Lightning suddenly flashes. Startled they suddenly separate.)

DARO *(heaving, picking himself up)*: This cannot be. We carry life and death in our pores yet we attempt to throttle ourselves without the presence of an enemy.

HARAPPA *(angered, perplexed)*: Where is Asoka, where does he travel when the Sun falls from space, to where does he vanish when the constellations exhibit?

DARO: I cannot speak to the levels that confine you.

(Each of them now standing, again, at angles to one another.)

HARAPPA: So I'm nothing but black salt to scatter amidst this climate of enigma. You seem lost inside some unknown brokenness, in a diagram with your primal forces missing.

DARO *(confidently)*: Sind has ascended far beyond visibility.

HARAPPA *(forcefully)*: Sind is the world. Sind rises and is a force like the Sun. Sind transfixes light. *(Looking warily in all directions)* You hide Asoka from me. If Asoka remains hidden all of Sind will rebel, then the astrologers will pronounce your nerves as poison.

DARO: You renounce your own reasoning. So it's the astrologers who now hold you. You dissemble and drown your own powers in heavenly blizzards.

HARAPPA *(as if arguing his case)*: You seek to confuse my statement by falsely commingling its content with the plane of the un-provable *(Pause)* You mine a harried moment so as to create justification for your distorted point of view.

DARO *(slightly raised voice)*: No Harappa, murder no longer persists as a means. You seek to implant our former goals and anoint our previous fables.

HARAPPA *(begins to circle Daro again)*: How does he ignite when the oneiric comes and claims him?

DARO: So I've conspired with dark magicians to dissipate his form in uncharted caves.

HARAPPA: Daro, you conspire on the plane of dangerous hibernations.

DARO: Asoka rules! He has balanced the affairs of both land and blood. He has weighed the coffers. He has surveyed the soil.

HARAPPA: Yet you do nothing but protract fumes. There is nothing at this stage you can account for.

DARO: I'm accounting for the present condition of things.

HARAPPA *(hands behind his back)*: Forever the prevaricator.

DARO: I've told you Asoka is not missing.

HARAPPA: Then to where has he travelled? To some apparitional mountain? Or does he remit to a region where the oblivious swallows him whole?

DARO *(staring intently at Harappa)*: You bait, you bait, and you bait again. You jaundice the circumstance. You attack from constriction.

HARAPPA: I've created no demands. Asoka is missing and the table of power is now abstracted.

DARO: When inner rays extend their power from within you, you will cease to display threat and any form of threat.

HARAPPA: As if my presence consists of treason. Therefore you turn my thoughts to your own making. Say, I tell you that the Sun has different phases, you would distort my summation to such a degree that several solar locales would appear inside one broken moon. Then, according to your thinking the Sun would appear as one perpetual night.

DARO: The coffers are in order!

HARAPPA: Now you reverse yourself and seek to mollify my presence.

DARO: I've never reduced you, you…

HARAPPA *(interrupting)*: According to you lakes blow in as mirages, and moons disappear and leave no trace on the sands.

DARO *(exasperated, holding up his hands)*: You place burden where none can be placed.

HARAPPA: No Daro, you move pieces of abstraction all the while plying your thoughts concerning silver you will gainfully extract from Sind. Exchanging with you is like trying to extract a mongoose from its movement.

DARO: You hate the light that passes through you.

HARAPPA: All I hear are deficits uttered from you. You fail at concretizing smoke.

DARO *(forced laughter)*: You mean smoke that issues from divination.
HARAPPA: You're stumbling Daro.

DARO: So Asoka will grant you punishment of me. He will permit forced labour from my limbs.

(A racket of crows becomes audible. Both men stare at one another as if

the crows were signaling omens.)

See, Asoka sends us signs, he sends us forces that reflect in us as mirrors with forms.

HARAPPA: You've fixed Asoka at some unalterable level who magically casts crows from some strange interregnum…

DARO *(breaking in)*: You doubt and disrespect!

HARAPPA: As a person who kills I simply register bodies all other possibility has ceased to exist.

DARO: Because you understand perfect strategy as homicide you've failed to grasp Asoka's proto-heightening.

HARAPPA: You patronize, and seek agreement for annihilation of physical law! All you do is summon abstraction. There's no fact of limit with you!

DARO: How do you define limit?

HARAPPA: It's clear!

DARO: Known dimensions, the bifurcation of life and death!

HARAPPA: Of course, life and death exist as universal schism. *(Pause)* You make it seem as if I were a stranger to my own thinking. *(Beginning to circle Daro once again with a tone of accusation)* You desire to dissolve me, to cast aspersion upon my thinking.

DARO *(almost dismissive)*: You gorge yourself upon old density. The past can never fully animate itself. Asoka…

HARAPPA *(smouldering)*: You conspire with the unseen. *(He stops*

29

circling Daro) You whisper assassinations through his mouth, you tie up corpses in his sleep.

DARO: You malignantly imply that I'm attempting to kill you. Yet it was you who attempted to unsheathe your sword. *(Pointing at Daro)* It is you who have hurled the imprecations at Daro the dwarf goat, of Daro with his horns unfurled!

HARAPPA *(intently)*: As a Minister of War you must know something of pillage, of how crops are killed, of how armies are starved and drained.

DARO: So I'm treasonous, I've failed to drain blood, I've failed by listening to whispers from lizards. *(Turning quickly and moving face to face with Harappa)* I always get the sense of Saturn rising from your humours. You've...

HARAPPA: Of course I've killed for the greater good. How can I be faulted for confronting a carcass within battle and casting it back into sulphur?

DARO *(backing away)*: I carry no disrespect Harappa. You've weakened all our foes, you've kept the Aryans at bay. I have no desire to plague Sind with defeat.

HARAPPA: Then why do you doubt me as I have served Asoka so well? I've given him the power to extend his hands above and adroitly seize ravens...

DARO: So you credit yourself for keeping Asoka protected, for emitting great value to the land, but another phase has come upon us.

HARAPPA: You're unveiling omens.

DARO: You want answers, you want letters from jurisdiction, you want portions of thought instantly definable.

HARAPPA: Life and death are definite. They never cease to replicate themselves.

DARO *(begins walking back and forth holding his hands behind his back)*: Everything is separate for you Harappa. Nothing can ever contain its living opposite at once.

HARAPPA: I've seen spiders who've guided themselves as if they were soldiers crossing deserted expanses. Asoka knows that I've wrought unpredictable stratagems. I've woven rumour as emphatic distraction, all the while brokering antonyms of balance. You, above all, have witnessed the outcome of bodies.

DARO: I need no convincing. What I'm saying to you is that the winds have shifted.

HARAPPA: So human value has shifted. Let me ask you Daro, has its value ceased to breathe or imbibe? Has it ceased to argue and reproduce itself? Maybe you are the exception who is able to extract the substance-less from air.

DARO *(agitated)*: I brew internal ore…

HARAPPA: Then you are a leper who feasts on magic.

DARO: Other levels have evolved Harappa.

HARAPPA: So this is mining that the body can't see.

DARO: Yes! *(Pause, then circling Harappa)* You argue as would an Aryan. You build doubt, as if we continued to struggle for ice and gold. And so you doubt that Asoka can supersede visual definition.

HARAPPA: What you continue to do is to solicit strangeness, all the while you dissemble like a treacherous crawler, like some scorpion

31

attempting to transmute into a hawk to pierce the Sun. *(Pause)* You're deadly Daro. Yet you try to camouflage poison and present yourself as mirage, as flotational yogin, as some strange Kemetic scarab.

DARO *(stunned, stopping in mid circle, stung to the quake)*: I've offered no accusation, or posed no threat to your ascendancy. *(His voice gaining strength near the end of the sentence)*

HARAPPA *(tone of accusation)*: You've accused me of projecting intolerable harm, of protracting violent and inconsequent judgement, of being possessed by a base impure intelligence.

DARO *(in a more conciliatory manner)*: You've questioned me about Asoka, and I've cast rays upon his transparency. He rises out of hell when the moon wanes. He vanishes in order to retrieve his blood from tyrannical consumption.

HARAPPA: You pontificate Daro. You surreptitiously engender my cause with disfavour, you strangle my ascendancy in your wake.

DARO *(annoyed)*: How do I deny you? By casting you in a role of un-gained performance? By whispering to Asoka to disregard your achievement?

HARAPPA *(stridently)*: I am First Minister...

DARO: It is not about being First Minister, or procuring only ancillary rank.

HARAPPA: So rank is nothing. Asoka had no plan...

DARO: His old plans are ash, they are ghosts now brewed in cauldrons of emptiness.

HARAPPA: I have the honour of his word, my appointment has been sealed in blood.

DARO: I've never denied you rank, no one has denied you. You remain, next to Asoka, the first born in battle. You have brought the best of Sind to our burning tribal lake. Asoka has titled you "Immortal Lion of Battle." Your command has been ferocious.

HARAPPA: Then why do you plague me with skills I don't possess.

DARO (*almost magisterial*): We know the beauty of the "Great Year", and because we know the beauty of the "Great Year" our skills need be lifted to other levels of matriculation.

HARAPPA: So I'm ignorant of these matters and can only advance through terminal quaking.

DARO: The respect you've garnered is never prone to wavering. This is why I've refused you concubines on the eve of battle. You descend on the enemy like hail. They feel the wrath of your form and witness the purity of your appearance.

HARAPPA: Daro, you both praise and betray me all in a single stroke. I can never tell if you've coerced the archers into haunting me.

DARO: The planes have shifted…

HARAPPA: You repeat yourself…

DARO: Birth and death have gone blank…

HARAPPA: Again I ask, how can Asoka fail to appear?

DARO: He is apart. He no longer glows in the atmosphere.

HARAPPA (*insistent*): I will speak to him at dawn.

DARO: He is beyond Harappa. He is marking his movement through the twelve gates of darkness.

HARAPPA *(scornfully)*: You're telling me he's dead, that he moves as disembodiment.

DARO: Things need be understood Harappa, things need be understood.

HARAPPA *(walking back and forth with an agitated gait)*: You present no proof, you present no palpable presentation for neither voice nor eye. You stress his non-formation, you stress Asoka's horrific functional absence as if all motion from order had vanished. So in this state I've become a central peculiarity, only capable of scooping dust, of remaining ignorant of what I now must do.

DARO: We are more than primal hominids, more than primal compounds capable of registering injury. Believe me Harappa, I refuse to pander to estrangement, to violence that only scatters mirages. I've never ordered you to describe Asoka in my image. What I can say is that he ascends and descends inside his interior divagation.

HARAPPA: The manner by which you convey yourself no longer casts substance. It's as if you are incapable of fever. What are you Daro, some post-mortem functionary, some in-seminal form of meta-hieroglyphics living without basis? *(Pause)* Even if you plunged your hand through fire I have no sense that it would burn. It's as if your formation has become glass. If I throw my dagger at your form it will only chip your ribs in portions.

DARO: We are merely entities in passage.

HARAPPA: No Daro, it is only you who have been pronounced by absence and you expect the Sun to tutor your own negation.

DARO: You demean without basis. *(Philosophical tone)* Let me say that there are cycles of breathing I now perform that can never be verbally objectified.

HARAPPA: Which means you are privy to being seared as property, to being handled by blinded hands, to being cajoled by impalpable symbols.

DARO: I've never said as such. You fabricate, as if I arose from deceptive embalming…

(Harappa interrupts Daro by performing exaggerated hand gestures resembling pentagrams in the air.)

DARO: What are you attempting to do, block me by making signs in the air?

HARAPPA: I'm sculpting axes. Since you know the signs that lead to the infinite you must recognize what I've suggested. They carry little power. Have the birds trembled and fallen from flying? Has the wind ceased its motion? I am not here to regale you or to express…

DARO: Hesitations Harappa, nothing but strategy as hesitation.
HARAPPA: Asoka has not disappeared. So where do you hide him? On the median plane? In a garden of circles? Or does he hover in the bloodless hearts of magicians?

DARO: So to you, he's partially shifted, imperfectly occulted.

HARAPPA: You mock and you mock again. You enkindle storms. You fail to suture your own alignment. You fail to engender the uranian.

DARO: I am only speaking of magma that inspires true journey that allows fragments to cohere. Remember, Asoka embodies translucence in his speech.

HARAPPA: Then summon him to speak. Let him assemble his flames before our eyes.

DARO *(shaking his head)*: I can give no visible proof.

HARAPPA: When you turn around in circles he vanishes, he negates his own plurality. His cells have dispersed, he wanders across blizzards without trace.

DARO: There are higher forms that inhabit the body. There are cycles that perplex the common purview.

HARAPPA: So now the Emperor exists as impalpable tiger. So now he hunts as a subset of action, as a hungered flame swallowed by his own darkness.

DARO: So how can he threaten his own blood? How can he assault the very fire that protects him?

(Harappa starts frantically pacing, grasping for orientation, then suddenly stops.)

HARAPPA: I've never accused him of plotting against his nature. No, I have not said this Daro. Instead you've goaded me, you've rankled the blood thirst in my mind and I've reacted. As trained killer I respond to every form that reacts. Believe me. I am aware of all the murmurs that leak, of all the enemies who thrive and eventually intercept themselves. In this sense I am sensitive to all noise, to all suggestion that interrupts pattern. *(Pause, a-lit with a new idea)* You've hidden Asoka in a pitch room, you've created a tenebrous hiding zone…

DARO: You manipulate Harappa, you reduce, you comfort yourself by harangue.

HARAPPA: So what if I harangue, and break you in two like a bushel. Perhaps I will seize you and have you salted and placed in a hive of rapacious dragons. As if my mind had been reduced to such a degree that it could create legislation for something as childish as the slaughter of ants.

DARO: No, but you seem capable of aligning with snakes.

HARAPPA *(Pointing to himself)*: This is weaponry atop a blue camel ejecting javelins from his heart.

DARO: You blind the Sun…

HARAPPA: You're the magician. How do you so miscast language?

DARO: I am never separate from its fumes, and because I am not separate from its fumes, Asoka, nor his lions, nor his scarabs can ever roam as separate fragments.

HARAPPA: So now you consider yourself something other than a living person. I, who've brushed blood away from your eyes, who've created with you perfect strategies for slaughter…

DARO *(averting Harappa's glance)*: Asoka has cleansed his thoughts of death. He's open to new elements of living.

HARAPPA: So now I'm the immortal boar that he's left behind!

DARO: To know the effect that Asoka now casts must hone an alchemy of terror in your heart.

HARAPPA: I know I have killed, and sparked undue erosion. I ask for no forgiveness, for no relief from agitation.

DARO *(abruptly)*: We've broken beyond the plane of agitation, and cleansed the living field of great blinding, so much so that compassion now flares…

HARAPPA: Asoka…

DARO *(cutting him short)*: He's developing precepts, he's opening moons in his heart.

HARAPPA: So do these moons divide ether from the blood? Do they emit from their forces ethics of war? Do they properly ignite a functioning Imperial system?

DARO *(exasperated)*: All you do is evoke doubt and lessening. It's your perpetual posture.

HARAPPA: So I've been bred for immolation, for corrupted assignation.

DARO: You cease to let yourself breathe, you un-plot your own purpose.

HARAPPA *(quick rejoinder)*: I mold sand, I sculpt dust, I monitor the drinking of potions.

DARO: I do not advocate secretive fumes from neutrality, or spontaneous dissolution of the Aryans.

HARAPPA *(trying to self-convince himself)*: I remain the First Minster of War!

DARO: Asoka ingests the moon. New balances have arisen.

HARAPPA: Living and dying have not ceased…

DARO: I am not denying nature nor am I summoning some subjective form of agitation to ensnare you. I'm simply marking life as non-arrival with itself. *(referring to himself)* I have no power to author the various leanings of the zodiac, nor can I be pointed out as the principle author of death. As for the cooking of curses, never has such intention crept inside my thinking.

HARAPPA: You know all too well the pressure that compounds wounds.

DARO: You bring up old scars.

HARAPPA: You know the moans, the mothers begging…

DARO: Asoka has risen...

HARAPPA *(Interrupting)*: Is he Horus? Does he aspire to the realm of the bodiless RA? Does he sum up the whole confoundment of space?

DARO: How can he feign his realia as immortality? As if he has surmounted the unbearable in being. *(Looking down at his own hands)* He is simply freeing himself.

HARAPPA *(laughing)*: So Asoka is this ghost who attempts to improve us, who softens our coarseness, and makes us pliable as wind.

DARO *(slowly looking upward)*: He's reaching for other realms.

(Lightning flashes twice. Not startled, the two raise their heads as if to take note and then return to facing one another.)

HARAPPA: So since he ascends how does his architecture enkindle? Is his throne alit by sudden carbon and gold? Does his shield now flash with the essence of RA? *(Pause)* Or has he now abandoned his subjects as an absented god? Perhaps he now sails across a superior sea.

DARO: Since you tinge me with absence, I remain rife with proto-regicide. Perhaps you will celebrate my downfall by roasting living boars amidst the fog of the peaks.

HARAPPA: You plot as if igniting all the figments of chess.

DARO: No, it is you that does nothing but think his own thinking. You pile up bones in a circle.

HARAPPA: So since I remain the Prince of Death, I rule nothing other than an empire of figments. To you I am a formless autocrat who legislates negation. I've never lost my respect for limits.

DARO: And what are your limits? The spilled blood? The throttled babies?

HARAPPA *(forcefully)*: Lands need be annexed!

DARO: But…

HARAPPA: If you fail…

DARO: The living can no longer commune with darkness. *(Pause, emphatic)* Have the dead ever spoken through you?

HARAPPA *(restrained laughter)*: You usurp Asoka's juridical propensity.

DARO: I am simply responding to the dark that leaps about you. The contorted power in your voice, all the terror that misnames you.

HARAPPA: So what then is my name? How do you account for my initial natal direction? Perhaps, I am like Asoka, an albino slipping between different dates.

DARO: I'm seeing other formations, other principles of slippage. Because you are white with slaughter…

HARAPPA *(holding his hands to his face)*: See I am perfectly resonant. No blood has drained. I remain red and red African!

DARO: I have no doubt of the rays that suffuse your skin. We are both rife with these rays.

HARAPPA *(impatient)*: Your mind revolves, you tell me nothing! What about trade, what about our dock at Lothal?

DARO: Trade is stable and has never curtailed. Our people thrive and are cleansed of fatigue.

HARAPPA *(proceeding to walk in a tight circle, head downward)*: Why do you always sustain such immaculate misgiving?

DARO: I've only referred to other states of comprehension.

HARAPPA *(head suddenly raised stilled in one position)*: You scatter the catastrophic, you sum up spoiled bread, you always whisper through judgement.

DARO: You are bitter because…

HARAPPA: Because I am an ailing old lion with no new blood to drink!

DARO *(intensely)*: There are canyons between us!

HARAPPA *(almost calmly)*: To you Sind is nothing but vapour, nothing in the main except philosophical debris *(Pause)* Asoka has told me nothing. Does he scorch his script by means of the wind? Or do the scarabs now descend as his counselors? Perhaps he tells the bulls to crush his private maze.

DARO *(deadly quiet in his voice)*: You stagger Harappa and you know it.

(The stage suddenly dims another level. Harappa begins moving in different directions flailing his sword at emptiness. After several seconds the dimmed stage brightens to its former strength.)

HARAPPA *(looking up into the heavens)*: Asoka! Asoka! Asoka!

(He then falls to one knee. All the while Daro has remained stilled. His emotion turned inward.)

HARAPPA *(looking up at Daro)*: So now you've claimed the superior position. I am nothing other than a bedazzled entity, nothing other than a bedazzled pontoon lost out at sea.

DARO *(quiety, standing in an almost commanding position)*: I've never made claim to superior reason.

HARAPPA *(slowly standing)*: No, you battle me as if I were some malformed creature suddenly ascended from the grave.

DARO: You create partitions, you hallucinate your own summons.

HARAPPA: Of course I smoulder, of course I command my own assignation.

DARO: The corpses you've buried no longer have fate.

HARAPPA: You create conspiracy as if I've orchestrated bones in a universal graveyard.

DARO: So I'm casting your body in a forge to be consumed.

HARAPPA: You carry things too far as I've waged war against the known constellations *(Pause, paternalistic in tone)* I protected you. I allowed you to engage slaughter without the pressure of known leadership.

DARO: I am neither dominant nor am I weakened.

HARAPPA: I...

DARO *(breaking in)*: As for me, I've refused the need for death, for its chronic subjugation.

HARAPPA: What does Asoka say since you've found your way through the maze of his animus. It seems you've captured the scent of his electrical intensity. You know his glossary of vipers and how he's drained them. You know the power of his previous anger and. . .

DARO: And now I can no longer measure myself by absolutes. As if we could know the Sun without living motion, without its revolving in space.

HARAPPA *(marked concentration)*: You imply that birth is none other than protracted invisibility.

DARO: Asoka will not fail. He has studied fire from the great elliptical forests. He has studied levitation of terrain into number.

HARAPPA *(throwing up his hands)*: So now you know God, and are capable of bending forces. And is Asoka God? Does he quench his impalpable hunger in heaven? *(Pause)* So is this the state of royalty? It's nothing but confused estrangement.

DARO: I repeat, he no longer confirms himself through prior legality.

HARAPPA *(perplexed, angered)*: Again, you define my effort as prior obligation, as something that addresses old motives. Perhaps I am a dragon on a boat, or a hostile sheen upon waters. So indeed, I must impede Asoka's charisma.

DARO *(quietly)*: He has not left you Harappa, nor does he seek to invade your blood with incurable perdition.

HARAPPA *(heightened voice)*: So does he evince himself behind the moon? Does he rise and wander across the maps in his heart? Does he row up and down the river of his veins?

DARO: All is internal. He has spoken of sonic deltas in his sleep. He has known osmotic stars that rise. He knows the Green Sun of the spirit.

HARAPPA: Can such a sun be weighed? How and when does it bring forth its rays?

DARO: All that one can say is that we exist on terra/luna.

HARAPPA: You're deceptive and you malign, attempting to scatter my mind with distraction.

DARO: Asoka follows no roads...

HARAPPA *(interrupting)*: There exists no evidence of his travels. *(Beginning to circle Daro again)* So what does Daro hear? What does Daro envisage? Have all our slaughters been for nil? What of our trained falcons? Do they continue to fly as density? Do they dig up parts of flesh? Do we remember their moving scrolls across the sky?

DARO: They remain part of the great rhythm.

HARAPPA: What rhythm? Listening to owls bleed. Watching moons go blank in the brambles.

DARO *(pointing in the distance)*: Go to Lothal and listen to the moon send waves into shore.

HARAPPA: You mystify. You sculpt deceit from astrological pylons. *(in a threatening tone)* You ration splinters inside my nerves, you make my waters run thin. *(With a loud voice)* Ignite Asoka, bring his image before me!

DARO *(quietly)*: I remain sans the power of our old magicians.

HARAPPA: Then summon them, bring his body back from limbo!

DARO: You are the only one who pronounces him as dead. You provide no possibility for his hovering, for his body to respire as symbol.

HARAPPA *(almost mocking)*: Then he sleeps at night on the sun. Perhaps he has commanded the lightning to stop.

DARO: You mock because you disbelieve your own condition.

HARAPPA *(very aggressive)*: And you can tell me of my condition, of my stains, my emotions, my pointless self-refusals.

DARO: I've only responded to your verbal assemblage. You've risen above martyred sands, you've opened up gusts of turbulence, and I've listened to the ghosts make noise in your veins.

HARAPPA: Which means you bequeath no judgement on yourself. Which means you are to scheme and gamble against yourself in order to assume commanding position.

DARO: You seem to confirm your own embranglement.

HARAPPA: You thirst on your own insistence. You drink a glossary of nebulas.

DARO: So since I hatch claws, and rampage through Asoka's power, what naturally follows is that I purposefully vilify dead bodies!

HARAPPA: You openly attack my personality. And since I am not your personality I do not stand beside you to christen your position, or abduct your circulation. *(Pause)* If you seek to withdraw, you seek to withdraw.

DARO: I meditate by means of mantra, by means of inner rotation, I've never cancelled activity by omission.
HARAPPA: It seems you author your own conspiracy.

DARO (*starting to pace again*): Your shadow looms at the level of dust and bricks.

HARAPPA: You make of Sind an untenable exhibit.

DARO: Then overthrow the Sun and let the constellations randomly migrate. Since you failed to calculate magnificence…

HARAPPA: I've released no power in my claims. I've laced no doctrine with poisoned animation.

DARO: You emit your doctrine every moment that you breathe. You re-invigourate blind force, you seek to truncate new beginnings.

(*Harappa's eyes roll back, he seems to stagger as if some other force had entered his bloodstream.*)

HARAPPA (*as if dreaming*): For each man to slay a lion on his voyage, to slay each and every serpent that he captures, so that he is capable of inventing a darkened solar noon, so that he staggers at the tomb of his gressorial essence, making huts as property by dissection, to bless new burial in war, to slake my thirst through python's hearing, to kill and be absolved of that killing…

(*Harappa begins to reel as the stage grows imperceptibly dimmer, streaked by shafts of red light. Daro begins to balletically circle the staggered Harappa, who attempts to wave his arms and make incoherent signs with his hands. Again, Harappa falls to one knee as if gasping for air. The stage slowly darkens.*)

ACT II

AN AVALANCHE OF REFRACTION

The stage suffused by partial light. Three figures sit in a semi-circle stilled in meditative posture staring into blankness, holding awls, as each inscribes three small bowls with indecipherable markings. In the background there is a mantric drone of sistrums and bells. They begin speaking in unison:

THE THREE MAGICIANS (*in unison*): He is riding in his darkened uranian boat across the twelve postures of the zodiac.

He is tested by all manner of embranglement.

He is raising himself to greater power.

He sails to greater joy through the wrath of danger.

He survives by transmuting rain out of poison.

He infuses its darkness with incessant regality.

Chariots from the Sun now race in his veins.

The macabre no longer swallows him.

His pedestals have vanished. His weight has disappeared.

Fire now roars as his matter.

This is Asoka.

This is Asoka.

This is Asoka.

(The stage goes briefly dark quickly followed by three flashes of green light. The stage goes dark again, and returns to its original dimness. The Magicians are now standing three-quarters turned to one another, all the while casting sidelong glances to the audience.)

FIRST MAGICIAN: Asoka prolongs his stay concerned with nether occupations. He conjoins with nether modes of the Sun.

SECOND MAGICIAN: It is a glossary of brick that blazes.

THIRD MAGICIAN: Onyx scorches his blood and re-returns to his lair. *(Pause)* He is nascent in his findings.

FIRST MAGICIAN: He leaks other apprehensions.

SECOND MAGICIAN: He no longer works in error.

THIRD MAGICIAN: This is why he ceases killing. The Sun now shines as his balance.

FIRST MAGICIAN: He scatters salt. He speaks through mirages.

THIRD MAGICIAN: This is why he cannot take form or create himself as image.

(A figure in white suddenly appears with a bowl that smoulders, placing it at the feet of the First Magician.)

FIRST MAGICIAN *(closing his eyes, with reverent tone of voice)*: He struggles with self-wrought illusion.

SECOND MAGICIAN: He rings inclement bells.

THIRD MAGICIAN: He listens to tigers encroaching.

SECOND MAGICIAN *(hands prone position)*: He's starting to understand shadows as they emerge from water.

FIRST MAGICIAN *(eyes still closed)*: It seems he's collapsing in 3 fires.

(The ghostly figure reappears and circles the Magicians and disappears.)

THIRD MAGICIAN: It seems he's sculpting lions from transcendental kindling.

SECOND MAGICIAN *(gripped with a kind of tremor)*: He's resurrecting bodies who've suffered death from random ordinal blows.

FIRST MAGICIAN *(igniting circular movement)*: Saffron now spills from his pores.

SECOND MAGICIAN *(moving in tandem with First Magician)*: He rings great bells with his vision.

FIRST MAGICIAN *(in movement as well)*: He knows that the Sun is blue at dawn.

(Movement continues. They now begin to chant their words.)

SECOND MAGICIAN: He no longer clings to tempestuous serpents.

THIRD MAGICIAN: Dust no longer decides him.

FIRST MAGICIAN: He is liberty invaded by mantras.

SECOND MAGICIAN: Because he de-resists himself he rides lions across the Sun.

FIRST MAGICIAN: He returns and remains hidden inside the Sun.

IN UNISON: The lions are both living and dead and are neither. Asoka is both living and dead and is neither. He ascends above the field of interior tension, above spillage from locusts and fever. His sands exist as seeming optimal mirrors. They exist as rivers of diamonds, as impalpable policies. He now and again cloaks himself as cunning raptor and exists as light between functionless states. Through blind ordeal, monsters vanish…

FIRST MAGICIAN *(his voice rising above the chorus)*: We are chariots parted by flame cajoling ourselves out of death. Our very eyes being solar forms and moons that magically ignite as inscrutable peregrinations.

(Speaking in trance like succession.)

FIRST MAGICIAN: Forces.

SECOND MAGICIAN: Spells.

THIRD MAGICIAN: Empty traces as our blood.

FIRST MAGICIAN: Sleep without negative gain.

SECOND MAGICIAN: Our shadows do not sleep in his midst.

FIRST MAGICIAN *(shaking his head, eyes violently blinking)*: He is sitting with his lions in a condor's palace. He being the colour of black diorite, his lions being partially blue, his condors bright red.

52

SECOND MAGICIAN *(holding up his arms, turning his hands back and forth)*: I've hidden mirrors in my skin that reflect him striding through smoke and dark.

THIRD MAGICIAN *(holding his hands over his eyes)*: The Sun is perfect medicine inside his eyes.

FIRST MAGICIAN: He has absolved a harmful era of itself no longer prone to powers of sulphur.

IN UNISON: Now the uranian gulls have begun to brilliantly hover. And because they hover we cannot name them, or extract from them laws according to physical motion. Perhaps one of the gulls will be named Asoka wandering consumptive ranges, his voice converted to starlight, leading the others through the Sun that refuses him speech. Yes, they are alchemical gulls, because the Sun itself has come from nothing.

FIRST MAGICIAN: Asoka amidst this eclipse listens to sonic fevers. And some descend on him knowing as they know that the universe existed before it existed. Though he is gull he pre-exists the gull, who fore-tells himself as gull, who pre-evokes his own endurance. In this dimension he both walks and rises, and appears and disappears as higher dimensional translucence…

(Stage briefly goes dark pierced by streaks of light. Then just as quickly the dimmed lighting resumes.)

FIRST MAGICIAN: He is both amidst and apart, he, who no longer connives or disrupts, or is open to evil.

(The Magicians still themselves and face the audience and are suddenly circled by the figure in white who empties smouldering water at their

53

feet and disappears stage left. As he disappears bells begin imperceptibly ringing in the background.)

FIRST MAGICIAN: He preaches to himself by adding nullification by means of ruses and ciphers, and diameters that go blank.

THIRD MAGICIAN *(eyes rolling up in his head)*: He is incandescence that soars.

SECOND MAGICIAN: He has dispersed the fort of myrmidons. He has transcended their seed through volcanic fog.

FIRST MAGICIAN: He is paradox by black powder.

SECOND MAGICIAN: He is the ore of the Sun.

THIRD MAGICIAN: He carries the power of all known habitation.

IN UNISON: The rawest dignity of light, a phantom lion roaming a porch of scorched silver, now he sails into Lothal in a boat of blue scarabs. He has cast himself beyond the power of infernos as he carves his notes on an astral mason's table, as sigil he exists as unstable ether, as fledgling tourmaline body, rising to light by rising further into light, seeping beyond his own presence as diaphanous witness, as great electrical ascent, as roaming electrical migration.

SECOND MAGICIAN *(pointing to the heavens)*: Great sound resounds inside the oceans on the moon.

(The stage slowly brightens tinged by citron and red. The Magicians begin weaving in and out of one another.)

In Unison: Nor is he victim, nor is he butcher, nor is he victim, nor is he butcher…

(As they continue to chant this phrase the light begins to turn to a bluish-green. Then the dimness descends, as faint humming transpires mingled with sistrums. They return to sitting in their original semi-circle, the sistrums then quiet and they suddenly speak without warning.)

In Unison *(quietly)*: He of black Elysian palpability, of diamond soaked iron, of blaze within blaze, of steep and resonant spinning, knowing that the lakes blaze without burning, this being Asoka, who spins beyond visible comprehension. Let us knit his uraeus with light, let us sculpt from his shadow imperishable carbon, he being the river of distillate travelling moons, thus, he balances ghosts, no longer of the energy of conflict, he now confers with clouds, emerging from trans-functional mazes. *(The Magicians stand again and begin chanting)* He is light from the waters of Nun, he is cyclical flood, his body exists as a river of bells…

(Their voices slowly fade, and the stage darkens simultaneously with a faint ringing of bells.)

ACT III

IN THE HALL OF BALANCE

There is a swarm of activity in the throne room. At its centre sits an immaculately carved chair placed there for Asoka. The attendants are moving about in various directions to no seeming purpose. The stage is suffused with faint emerald light. The five attendants seemingly melt away as the stage slowly dims. A ghostly figure approaches the chair with measured movement. The stage brightens, a blue-green light is centred upon the throne chair. A syncopation of drums transpires rhythmically laced with bells. The stage again darkens and when the emerald light reappears Asoka is seen sitting on his throne chair, donned in an azure robe fixedly staring at some impalpable point. Harappa then enters with a kind of in-direction in his gait.

HARAPPA *(bowing, then standing a kind of pleading in his voice)*: Revered Asoka, you've returned to visibility. I've remained constant on your behalf as First Minister of War. I've stained the Sun with blood for you. Have I not invaded snakes and rid them from your gullet?

(Asoka suddenly waves his right hand signaling for silence. Harappa bows his head again.)

ASOKA *(softly)*: You must be able to quell the inclement in your spirit. There must exist balance. There must exist other somas beyond gold. The energy you once trampled has re-arisen and gained living direction. As sigil it carries in its wake dark and uneven ciphers. I know you have conspired to mount and ride steeds, but that concerns my former plane. I am concerned with forms of speech that staunch evisceration and bleeding. *(leaning forward)* You've come to me in pursuit of tangled adders hoping that I might provide you with instruments for mayhem and slaughter. I've listened to your spirit mutter accusing me of breaking away from soil, of blurring the stations of power, of casting my property into the emptiness of space. *(Sitting back in his chair)* If I could fill a ship with carnivores I would subvert its mission by absconding the prey for the length of its voyage. *(Pause)* I refuse to array myself with mystical stupefaction. Because I'm coiled by true transparency I feel the tensions you bear concerning scripts of carnage. You seek to embrangle spells, to take away mystery, to pose yourself through repetitive threatening. You seek to empty sundials of their movement, to conjoin our collective body to stasis and fatigue. I am no longer troubled by clarity, and since you remain beholden to despair, claim it, be beholden to its devastation, to the mental inferno that seeks to protect it. Know Harappa that the mind by which you challenge light is nothing other than a veiled raptor that you've stolen to foment instigation. I am not accusing you of crime and the transfixing of crime. *(He gestures with his hands to himself)* It was I who drained collective blood from Kalinga, it was I regaled the Sun with my own claims. Therefore, I willfully extracted doubt from my actions. *(Slowly bringing his hands down on the chair's rests)* Your allegiance has been no less than splendour. You enacted every element for my desire for conquest. You spurred death in spite of the sorrow that it cast, in spite of its morose dictation. All you've known is the aggravated cinder as the force of every deed. Yet this has failed to raise the Deccan Plateau. The clouds have ceased burning as my allies. They no longer hide my skill-full tortures beneath rain. It is plain to see I am still shadowed by remorse, no longer conquered by my own denial. My sorrow swelters. I am a lessened monsoon. *(Asoka stares into emptiness)*

HARAPPA *(un-bowing his head, visibly shaken)*: If all my desires have become treason…

ASOKA *(quietly)*: The severed hands, the gold you extracted from their mouths…

HARAPPA *(anxious)*: Since my efforts have failed, I feel forced to cater to the splintered stumps of my victims. I ask you Asoka, does Kalinga now claim me, am I now one of its shadows? *(Bowing his head again)*

Am I now foil for all the terrified? *(Pause)* If it is your wish Asoka, I will partake of the in-nominate, I will accede to its levels of blankness. *(He tenses his shoulders while uneasily moving back and forth within the arc of a taut semi-circle, exasperated)* I feel as if attempting to climb a wall of black crystal.

ASOKA *(solemn tone)*: You possess the complication of partially troubled compunctions. You have yet to evade your own prowess and its nervous capacity for ruin.

HARAPPA: So how do you now honour me?
(begins to aimlessly walk about) I feel stained by suspension. I've lost my compunction to plan for the future. I ask you master, where are my former listening dogs? Where are my darkened camels that once rose from the deluge? *(Pause)* I am voided master, I know that I am voided. I am an accursed fish excluded from water.

ASOKA *(leaning forward)*: Did I say I am revengeful of the power you display? Have I ever equated your strength with poisonous amphibians? I now cull forms from higher example. Not, Harappa, as death count, or pre-classified fumes spawned from dissension. I have never sought to pair you with rivalry, or place your energy within a pre-ordained coffin.

HARAPPA: But Daro continues to plague me, as if his authority of silver had overcome nouns of gold.

ASOKA *(sitting upright again)*: You misconstrue your own tenor. You've scrambled your own power and made it turn backward.

HARAPPA *(fingers pointed towards his own chest)*: So why do I feel so haunted with error?

ASOKA *(forcefully)*: I am not here to assuage.
HARAPPA *(almost defensively)*: Then master, why do I feel so mocked?

Then why does the Sun angle me to the zodiac of disfavour?

ASOKA *(sitting up in a more bracing manner)*: You fish for infernos.

HARAPPA *(struggling)*: I feel a conspiracy that favours Daro.

(Harappa suddenly pulls out a dagger and places it at his throat.)

ASOKA *(calmly, but forcefully)*: Put your weapon away. You polarize your own insignia.

(Harappa drops the dagger. A faint sound of clanging is simultaneously heard in the background. A chorus of feminine voices begins to emanate just above a whisper.)

CHORUS: He cuts blood from the branches
        And swings wood
        And cuts blood from the branches.

(Harappa begins turning his head in all directions attempting to seek the source of the sound.)

HARAPPA *(holding his hands to his ears as if straining to hear)*: You hear them master?

ASOKA: I've heard nothing Harappa.

HARAPPA: With all due respect master, I feel splayed, I feel my balance has been insidiously upended.

ASOKA *(rising from his chair)*: So you accuse me of spells, of an absence of honour?

HARAPPA: I'm only asking that you listen.

ASOKA *(sitting down again)*: The sky remains clear. I have altered no discipline. As if I've inflamed a tribe of skulls with my speech. *(intently staring at Harappa)* So am I hiding idolatrous structures, igniting cold wagons with flames?

HARAPPA *(trembling)*: I am harried master. It seems I annihilate my own reason through spilled plasma. *(Lightly thumping his chest his dagger falls to the floor going unnoticed for the moment)* I feel I have been betrayed and put in position of a sullen fragmentary doctor. *(Turning in a tight circle)* So now I am useless to you. According to you I allow evil to burn, I being nothing other than a rabid monster. Perhaps I am paradox who has plummeted from starlight, a cannibal who thrives from perfect inequity. I remain doctor of carnivorous divisiveness, of writhing both on earth and in hell. Me, in-celibate leakage, moral flame occluded by the abyss. So I claim and do not claim myself as precursor to nothingness. With me, all the lamps, all the prime forces are extinguished. According to the present state of things I've commanded by infection, by laws that always prosecute human termination.

ASOKA *(leaning forward and in a solemn tone)*: The 300,000 slain are mingled with your honour. Their voices have submitted to your struggle. I remain indebted to your boldness, to the strategies that you've woven. You've allowed me to transmute my spirit by means of its flaws. You've allowed me to renew my contact with the invisible.

HARAPPA *(standing still in front of Asoka)*: I know that I am hated. *(His head turning in all directions)* Why does Daro hide from me? Why do I see you both only on separate occasions?

ASOKA: In my former state I would have had you quartered and stabilized on a gibbet for the things you say directly and more so for the things you imply. It seems you accuse me of conspiracy, of injurious intent veiled by ambiguity. *(Pause. Briefly angered)* I remain king. I, who've carried the world by dark incendiary strength. I've remained the occulted draft, the wind sans signature or inferno.

HARAPPA *(calmly)*: So I'm the bull you needed to cast strength, to stamp out the waters, to construct the corpses that you've needed.

ASOKA *(contained anger)*: I no longer use death!

HARAPPA: I'm intelligent. Now I'm being eroded and denied the power of my former victories. *(Walking back and in front of Asoka looking blankly at the floor)* I directed your forces as if fevered by rays. All of them poisonous, combative, pulling, I surveyed Kalinga like an Eagle. I created victory from spoils. I forged lavas, empowered fevers, entranced the enemy with halos, and mirages, and spirals.

ASOKA *(continuing to quiver)*: I cannot accuse you of seething, or of adjusting your sight according to combative meridians. *(Leaning forward once again)* I can say Harappa, have you never bartered for lucre, for destructive waste, for criminal requisition.

HARAPPA *(standing still facing Asoka)*: So why do I feel ruined? Why do I feel ruined self-stranded in vapour?

ASOKA *(furtively glancing at Harappa's fallen dagger)*: I have never sought from you skill which I've sullied through false accusation, nor have I intended for you to feign yourself as a leper in order to increase the image of my strength.

HARAPPA *(again circling while speaking)*: Then why do I feel felled by erosion? I am the targeted black garment, the estranged assassin feeling blinded in the heart. *(Suddenly stopping in mid-movement he notices Asoka eyeing his dagger as if they were in the reflex of battle, looking at Asoka)* Why is my dagger so strange? It casts no animation. It cannot leap. It cannot form itself as serpent.

ASOKA *(struggles to keep his composure, almost distracted)*: I have willed nothing. I have never struggled against your completeness or maimed your inward space in order to gain composure.

HARAPPA *(gazing back and forth between his dagger and Asoka)*: Why then these glances?

ASOKA: I am only concerned with your fever of loyalty.

HARAPPA *(eyes opening wider)*: So now you test me for treason. *(shaking his head)* I feel poisoned by your need for power.

ASOKA *(suddenly springing from his chair with heightened voice)*: Khonsu, Khonsu!

(The stage suddenly goes black. Lightning-like streaks shot across its emptiness. The stage un-darkens and is suffused by a dim yellow light. Asoka is sitting in his throne chair staring upward. Harappa remains standing in front of Asoka, slightly stage right remaining focused on Asoka.)

ASOKA *(calm, but slightly distracted)*: The sky is sending us signals.

(A ghostly figure suddenly enters stage left, wearing a blackened headpiece atop which sits an emerald uraeus. It is wearing a white ground length tunic, with its face and its hands coloured aquamarine. He unfurls a scroll)

KHONSU *(reading from the scroll in a whispered regal tone coming up to*

65

Harappa): You are master of the morose, you emulate distance, ruled by swollen bodies which erupt with ubiquitous narration. Bodies, rife with a cult of forms, with necrotic instigation.

(Harappa overcome, takes several steps backward. The stage goes dark for several seconds, then re-ignites in dimness. Asoka has returned to his throne. Harappa stands, but visibly shaken. Daro suddenly appears entering stage right.)

DARO *(walking toward Asoka referring to Harappa)*: See Master, he has returned from pure cinder. He has become our solemn precursor. He has returned from the fallen.

(Harappa attempts to feebly survey Daro's position with his hands. Rumbling is heard. Then an ethereal music begins to emanate throughout the hall. The three characters seem to be imbued by suspension. A kind poise begins to enter the atmosphere. Asoka sternly beckons to Daro. Asoka remains calm. Harappa evinces a slight distraction as he struggles to regain his psychic balance.)

ASOKA *(turning towards Daro)*: Your words seem dulled like an un-cutting knife. You assume that the throne is occupied solely by the body, and me, being the body who rules has the power to cast your destiny via the positive or the negative. In your heart of hearts you carry Harappa's original position as your thinking. You conspire in your own way to mentally harangue him. *(Pointing to himself)* Asoka is not here to placate or to replicate the vital personality, but to understand that I now only partially appear on this plane.

(Daro partially bows his head while looking askance at Harappa.)

ASOKA: I cannot be predicted. And since I cannot be predicted, I ask myself what does power lead to? What does it gain as an overall prerogative? How can victory be gained through the violence of daggers? Believe me, I cull meaning from both your glances. I know fate seals and un-seals fortune.

DARO (*palms turned downward*): Master, I've had no plan for usurpation, absolutely nothing concerning use of ceremonial treachery.

ASOKA: Why do I suspect that this intent commingles with your power? You know in your immediate mind that I am sculpting the invisible body, that I am advancing inside its thoughts knowing all along when reckoning will return.

DARO (*wary of Asoka's next utterance*): I've never conspired or challenged your eyes so as to extract their power from the limitless.

ASOKA: Stop assuaging me Daro! Don't speak to me as if your voice surveyed a narrowly guided script.

DARO: (*pulls his dagger as if to cut himself*): Master, then examine my blood.

ASOKA (*stands*): Stop it!

(*Daro now seething with his own confusion glances at Harappa, the latter beginning to re-gather an inner balance, as if both were conjoined by accusation. Both Daro and Harappa seem magnetized by Asoka's eyes.*)

ASOKA (*focused intently upon the both of them*): You attempt to understand my actions from dissimilar misperception. You are as eagles clashing above a runic gulf of frenzy. I understand the strength that gathers in your soma as philosophical bitterness, as purified strain constricted to quintessence. *(Pause)* Do you grieve for Kalinga? Do you feel its sorrow eating inside you? Do you mourn for its graves of blood? I still sense inside your differing commitment base political etching. Of how the lands are drawn, of how largesse will extend itself according to each of your personal interests. I no longer engage in the slaughter of animals, nor do I gloat at those smitten by calamity. I have renounced politically authored calamity and its concomitant activity of useless slaughter. One must pay one's interior debt for "animate beings," one must animate tolerance, and, say, procure medicine for lions, and subsist upon thought as transparency. *(Pause)* I could renounce you both as being authors of disservice, of being depressive monarchs of murder and scheming.

HARAPPA: Then why do you commingle me with Daro? Why are my thoughts regaled as being bound to lower subsistence?

ASOKA *(emphatic):* One must abandon darkened personal motives, one...

HARAPPA *(breaking in)*: I've measured blood for you, I've laid dark trapping nets, I've starved lions on your behalf...

ASOKA *(turning to Daro)*: See how the language of old mirrors is stained, how its laws have been altered as forms of old imprisoning fire.

HARAPPA *(growing bolder looking at Asoka)*: You specify me as ruination since you know as you know by possessing the invisible. Because I have never gained its rungs, I'm accused of sipping old poison, of scrambling blood inside my thinking. *(Turning to Daro)* I cannot speak for him. It seems...

DARO *(angered)*: So I emulate negation as confused example! *(Pointing to Harappa and Asoka)* You both deny me! Now both of you declaim by your actions that I've failed to subtend general honour.

ASOKA (sternly): You have lessened your honour Daro.

DARO: So you admit confusion Asoka between causes and opininated sources of these causes, of the leprosy of intrigue, and the schisms malefically wrought by this intrigue.

ASOKA: These storms are behind me. You condense insubstantial negatives.

(Asoka seeking to restrain himself from former tendency to violence, all the while cognizant of his ministers having crossed appropriate boundaries. He stares into the circumstance as if witnessing a storm during its interregnum. He stares into the distance attempting to conjure in himself the balance of Maat.)

DARO (blurting out without warning): The corrosions, the insolence, the frustrations, the fire that erupts from iron, and the jasmine that invades me through ghosts. And so Asoka, if you force me to revert to old habit, to a drowning tiger foraging through slivers of twilight, it is an attempt to keep me scattered, to seal my fate inside reductive emotion. I have swam the Oxus, traded Lapis Lazuli in Afghanistan, prayed to cosmic stones at Dilman, and exercised psychic grasp by predicting in-coming rafts floating into Lothal.

ASOKA (staring intently at Daro): You are referring to powers other than yourself. (Asoka suddenly stands and waves his hands above his head, as thunder rumbles, as bells begin ringing, a shadow of wings crosses the stage, Harappa and Daro look upward, mystified.) This is not the power that I speak of. I could haunt the populace like a burning panther, and then sculpt the sand so that it resembles blackened owls, so that they in turn are routed by spectral hummingbird sorties. Since I am concerned with other forces that the body can't see, I know sorcery at the lowest level of comment, therefore I cannot posit conjecture, or wade into personal motive in order to suggest my own spirit.

HARAPPA: What do you mean? Mental squalls? Unbalanced abiding?

ASOKA *(in a lowered voice)*: Have you ever escaped your own encasement, or studied your flames in secrecy? *(Turning to Daro)* You've studied in cellars of peril, beneath oceans of ancient chronology.

DARO: But…

ASOKA *(sitting down, then getting up, then circling his chair)*: It is to wish for nothing. Neither peril, nor bread, nor victorious rejoinder in battle, it is release from ubiquitous exposure, from storm clouds seeding the spirit. This being life that trembles beyond the state of mirage.

HARAPPA *(holding up his hands)*: How are my hands mirages? Why do I totter and turn ashen? Why is my blood partially stunned by unease? *(Pointing to himself)* As if my body were the equal of an abandoned flamelet. *(Now looking to Asoka)* As if I am no more than brushed tar on wood, no more than the fall of abrasive cinders.

ASOKA: You attempt to self-convince yourself.

HARAPPA: No, I am reacting to my own personal portion, to its form of limit that has erupted from every agony. *(on the verge of anger)* One is always breeched by the un-gainful, by being tangled in poison kelp.

ASOKA *(calm voice)*: Things must continue to be…

DARO: How can you…

ASOKA *(breaking in)*: We are always suspended Daro, we are sudden nouns in transition.

HARAPPA *(circling the both of them)*: Transition and quarrels and agony versus agony.

ASOKA: I utter neither false nor sculpted burdens. Imagine other planes than the body. *(He sighs)* You've both survived the maze of battle with its noisome moaning, with its commingling harassment. You see, I continue to test myself at this pitch of nervous purity. For you, Daro, it is like seeding umbilical hail, and for you Harappa, it is like watching a tribe of camels vanish into the sand.

HARAPPA: Then who is to say that you are master? Perhaps it is power from burnt speech, from chaotic in-sensation.

ASOKA *(seeming to restrain himself)*: So if I conceived drought as saturated bait, you both would accuse me of ill wisdom. You both could say that I have ceased to form myself, and have made of myself a paradox of confusion. Perhaps speech has been partially corrupted, that it remains sound from an ill-fated raptor. All accusation could be mimed within my person and become in both your eyes a stray or whitened rat.

(Harappa now stilled, parallel to Daro, with Asoka walking back and forth in front of them reflectively.)

ASOKA: True, I can track human warrens across a cliff face, I know the light where horses turn olive and green, yet I remain at my core an uninhabitable circumstance. I glance about and only see the glare from impermanent cuttings.

DARO: It seems you defend yourself Asoka.

ASOKA *(ceasing to move)*: I am no longer he who defends himself, or makes himself the equal of his former limit. There can only be charisma according to absence. Therefore I no longer subtend tracing that emits carnivorous abstraction.

HARAPPA: So if your flames fly backward how can we beseech you?

DARO *(looking at Harappa)*: All the crows though they feast seem broken. *(Tearing off the amulet around his neck)* I am holding an amulet of new animals.

(Asoka then holds out his arms, with his palms prone, slowly raising them up and down. Bells faintly ring in the background, the stage darkens, Harappa and Daro disperse in opposite directions.)

ACT IV

IN THE DORSAL CHAMBER

SCENE I

(The stage is bathed in a diffuse red light.)

Harappa is lying on a wooden bench writhing between sleep and waking. He begins to hear moaning, along with the muted eruption of horses' hooves, the latter two sounds commingled with the sound of vultures gorging on torn flesh. He turns over and over attempting to find comfortable respite. He is still attired in his ministerial vestments. He suddenly sits up, wringing his hands as if agony had entered his body. Without warning random voices begin to susurrate, further unsettling him with an energy he has never experienced before. He rises up and circles the bench with his dagger drawn, hacking at the air so as to silence the voices. He again lies down on the bench. A drone begins to brew, not unlike an ominous raga, slightly shrill and out of balance. He evinces understated trepidation as four women, without notice, slightly encircle the bench, arrayed in blood stained tunics, pointing accusatory fingers at him, hissing. As the raga lowers in intensity, they begin to susurrate in unison "Butcher of babies" as an extended mantra. They are arrayed in crocodiles' heads, opening and shutting their mouths. He sits up and buries his head in his hands. The stage slowly darkens.

SCENE II

(Daro is wandering his chamber diffuse with bluish light. He is fraught with consternation. There is a wooden bench in the corner stage right. Near the centre of the stage there exists a low pine coloured table atop which sits an urn.)

DARO: Is Asoka testing my nerve? Does he attempt to balance my carcass with his newly acquired morality? Am I his ascendant prince reduced to the status of lynxes and bears? Am I now his subservient leper whose body has been consumed by fractious wool? In light of this circumstance must I take on sudden form that resembles evasion? Have I riddled myself through the glamour of piety? Have I gone no higher than matter evinced as reptilian scar? Does Asoka see my striving being akin to a storm of lice? Or do I remain his vacuous tormenter charging through vacant flame? Does my body still register through distance and time? Or does my spirit still linger in the soils of Kalinga? *(Pause, more certainty in his voice)* I feel Asoka burns with challenge in his blood. That he still inscribes his armour with lightning and diamond. Perhaps he still revels in haunted action, plagued by moral failure vis a vis the architecture of slaughter. Perhaps he has swam through death in order to reach the other side of the living Sun. Perhaps he replicates the nettlesome, the odd invalidated sigils that he draws from. Perhaps I've become to him an odd unlettered locust arising from a swamp of metal. Perhaps he is no longer Asoka. Perhaps he is now trans-human. Perhaps his former body now vibrates as discarded salt. Perhaps he has escaped what we presently consider to be the physical form. I can see the effects of his form floating as a devastating solar mass. I can sense that he possesses a burgeoning inner condition that is beginning to seep into eternity, that he is beginning to rescale that part of infinity we've come to know as death. Yet I've not been able to ascend above the chaos that beseeches me knowing that I don't know while knowing that I know. I sense he glows as a cleansed portion roaming between trees and other splintered fragments listening to ethers of the dead.

(The stage suddenly goes dark, Khonsu appears arrayed in a white tunic.)

KHONSU *(voice slightly amplified having a haunting type of tenor)*: Absolve yourself Daro. Your being is now arching. If its growth is painful then painfully grow. It is other than rock or salt.

(The lights blink. Khonsu deftly vanishes stage left. Bluish light is restored as Daro drops his head and fades into the background stage right. The stage goes dark. A cacophony of conch shells and whispers along with muted gongs and flutes, intermixed with a kind of proto-chanting. These shards of chanting build to a palpable vocal harmonic that builds through intervals as a periodic cluster, then a sustained harmony transpires as the stage brightens with diffuse blue light with the three magicians arrayed in black chanting while sitting in a semi-circle sans pine table and urn. Suddenly the first magician begins speaking.)

FIRST MAGICIAN: We've entered a world burning with visitation.

SECOND MAGICIAN: The beings that we witness are stags in disguise.

THIRD MAGICIAN: They are forms that parallel their own enigmas.

SECOND MAGICIAN: They are coiled by unprincipled secrecy.

FIRST MAGICIAN: They are birds that seem to spring and vanish into utter flight.

THIRD MAGICIAN: Perhaps bitterness?

SECOND MAGICIAN: Perhaps self-exposure by daylight?

FIRST MAGICIAN: Perhaps they are crops exposed to new moons?

(Silence then indecipherable whispering amongst the three of them. Without warning, the Second Magician splits apart from the group, moving stage left and begins speaking to himself.)

SECOND MAGICIAN: Drought seems suspended in drought and now the atmosphere is impalpably igniting itself. Daro seems to know this. He understands that the moon can ignite in broad daylight. I've sensed him staring at its flames as if he ignited it from a distance.

THIRD MAGICIAN *(remaining seated, staring into the audience almost answering telepathically)*: I know that he stares at himself and understands himself to be the zodiac illumined by partial and half hidden numbers. His only dialogue is colloquy with the abyss and he suffers, he can only generate blankness. The roof of the stars provides him no succor. He seems imperiled by dissension.

SECOND MAGICIAN: Asoka spurs him to great honour. He has opened his shield to face the unknown.

THIRD MAGICIAN: He attempts to barter with himself.

SECOND MAGICIAN *(having returned to the semi-circle)*: Harappa remains dazed and cannot conduct his own strategy.

THIRD MAGICIAN: Asoka has blessed him with knowing the pain of self-deception.

SECOND MAGICIAN: Harappa's eyes now hurt from contemplation.

FIRST MAGICIAN: He wrestles with the strategy of his only known position. In his mind he stumbles over lakes and mountains and now is unable to describe himself.

THIRD MAGICIAN: Asoka has confronted them with the absence inside of themselves.

SECOND MAGICIAN: They've lost the constancy of misused grammar.

THIRD MAGICIAN: The void now builds its shape inside their minds.

FIRST MAGICIAN: Nothing is certain.

THIRD MAGICIAN: Nothing is certain.

FIRST MAGICIAN: If they continue to speak from positional symbols they regress from higher growth.

THIRD MAGICIAN: They will fail to comprehend the osmosis of orality.

SECOND MAGICIAN: As they rise in true ascent they will cease to accuse themselves of carking positional stricture.

THIRD MAGICIAN: Do we point to a golden world, or to chaotic sensitive judgement?

FIRST MAGICIAN: Daro now roams the fire of inclement suspension.

THIRD MAGICIAN (*eyes glaring with a start partially standing*): I sense differences. Harappa continues to inwardly roam through storms of blood. He carries his own witness into vile and occulted chambers.

SECOND MAGICIAN: He attempts to ruin the Sun and seek momentary calm within the loins of Durga.

FIRST MAGICIAN: He opens old clauses.

SECOND MAGICIAN: He surmounts and dismounts old mental horses that once led him to victory.

FIRST MAGICIAN: This is the scope of an old leper in triangulated mourning.

THIRD MAGICIAN (*sitting again*): His nerves are irregularly routed seeing history with the eyes of a reptile or a panther. He's tangled blood inside a shipwreck.

FIRST MAGICIAN: Yet Daro harbours complete suspicion of himself. *(Pause)* He remains suspended between Asoka and Harappa as a dazed beacon floating out of port.

THIRD MAGICIAN: Asoka is a gust of blazing antlers. He culls light from a realm of unbelievable blinding.

(They begin to rise in unison as dark blue smoke fills the stage as they begin to speak in unison.)

IN UNISON: We have swam from the lake of blankness
        We have voided as our proof the circumstance of fate
        Understanding through nutation the burden of advanced
        dilemma

(They then begin to move in a circle chanting.)

The lake of blankness remains our struggle, the lake of blankness remains our struggle…

(They dark blue smoke evapourates and is replaced by a shaft of green light that then seems to consume them.)

SCENE III

(Asoka alone ruminating to himself amidst diffuse yellow light, slowly walking back and forth across the stage evincing in his motion contained intensity.)

ASOKA *(in continuous movement)*: I'm accused of having congress with the unknown, of spinning my mind and allowing it to blur. I am accused of possessing the deadly combination of jealousy and grace telepathically scrawling itself on cinders. I know I am the subject of insidious envy, I who have absolved myself of eviscerated lice, of explosive camels charging into battle. To my immediate circle I've become a pointless moral lector spouting truncated wisdom illusive verbal stricture. Perhaps I carry the private torch of the un-gainful, yet I do not doubt, nor carry energy that dispirits, or burns as kinetic foil. No I am beginning to elevate with the spirit of a newly woken eagle. Khonsu has annealed me to the sorcery of alchemical suns. Their blazes continuously purify my testament that now keeps me alive as solstitial ballast. Thus, sound continues to leap into my soma, by articulating circles, by floating beyond itself as occult generation. By means of its occulted body I will speak to Harappa at dusk.

(The stage goes dark.)

SCENE IV

(The stage continues to be lit in diffuse yellow light. Asoka is sitting in his throne chair. Harappa stands in front of him angled stage right.)

ASOKA *(leaning forward in his chair)*: I've summoned you so that you can explain to me your continuous relation to the carnivorous. Now it is time to explain your spirit, your aggressive moral ravens. As you must know at this juncture my presence is not solely conveyed by occupation of the body in palpable space. As for spells they are never restricted by the terseness of palpable authority, they can never be solely constrained by suspension in amulets, nor can they be solely judged by individual colour such as indigo or carnelian.

HARAPPA: I have no need to partake of self-defense. You need not express my presence as barren anomaly. If my presence is desired as a spectral form of absence then so be it. I will disappear across the outer limits to harvest tin with the Phoenicians.

ASOKA *(returned to his natural sitting position)*: I've not brought you here to tutor the direction of your destiny, or to sculpt a shrine of my image for you to submissively follow.

HARAPPA: You are telling me you have nothing to fear…

ASOKA: No, this summoning concerns the soul when it continues to generate debris. This is something other than the mischief that is death, this being something other than the rising and falling of bodies.

HARAPPA *(striding angrily back and forth)*: You imply that I remain debris, that my mantle of royalty amounts to trained killing, that I possess no capacity for life. *(Angrily)* It was you who ordered slaughter, it was you who fostered upon us the code of bravery, it was you who commanded the burning of doves in others' blood! I absconded all witnesses that harboured resistance against Sind, and now I am told that I am dispossessed of answers, that my body must surreptitiously ascend.

ASOKA: Of course there exist no answers.

HARAPPA *(stopping his motion)*: Yet, you've said it with insistence, Asoka, mend your former actions, bend the current of your fate.

ASOKA: You accuse me of creating methods, of making up demonstrative boulders, so as to annul every nuance of strategy.

HARAPPA: I feel you concertize with Daro to build Sind as a trans-functional encampment.

ASOKA *(quietly)*: Perhaps it is. Perhaps Sind is no longer a society carved from blind weight. *(Looking intently at Harappa)* When floating inside the Sun I cast through field after field after field and Daro appeared other than in the state that you know him. Saying this I cast no aspersion on you, or attempt to hold your body as a mental lion in an urn. I do not ask you to revere me as would a myrmidon, expected to keep his mind closed so that it revokes its own evolvement. Yet I ask you…

HARAPPA *(breaking in)*: You ask me to make fire from the impossible, to somehow steal fire from discredited magic.

ASOKA: Have I ever condemned you as a beast, or made reference to you as some distorted form of panther, or tried to kindle you in the role of a scripted cadaver, creating you as the subservient mean arrayed in battledress. *(Quiet intensity)* Yet I know, Harappa, that the Sun has fallen and now risen as Kemetic ferment. Perhaps you will attribute this to magic, or as some ancillary whisper casting spells over the script of your senses.

HARAPPA: You attempt through moderate consolation to beget spells so that the thought in my mind will scatter and betray me.

ASOKA: I weave no ill intent. I am the "Amulet of Nefer," I am "Amulet of the Serpent's Head," I am "Amulet of the Sun's Orbit," my power blazes as Menat.

HARAPPA *(skeptical)*: So Asoka renews himself every hundred thousand years. He passes through the null of oblivion, he ascends from the power of dead blazes.

ASOKA: You both mock and doubt from ignorance of the impalpable. You slur the essence of the field that is now open to you.

HARAPPA: This is the field that Asoka embodies? This is the power of sudden chariots crossing the moon?

ASOKA: I feel a certain poison in your thinking. It feeds a spate of snakes.

HARAPPA: So I'm forbidden to doubt the shortcomings of your lifetime. I can in no way comment on its cascades of darkness.

ASOKA *(magnanimous)*: You are free to explore your own shadows, to mine the power in your self-abandonment. I can only say that you play dice with the contiguous.

HARAPPA *(peering pointedly at Asoka)*: Do I threaten you? Do I harry you as astrological monstrosity? Perhaps I empty vipers into your sleep by ringing an odious bell with my thinking.

Asoka: It seems Daro has risen above the lower domains…

Harappa: You imply insult and dishonour…

Asoka: I am speaking of script as sacred nuance.

Harappa *(irritated)*: Then why do you protect me? Why do I remain in your eyes as some necessitous assemblage? Why do you preface my efforts with demons?

Asoka: This is why we now convene as a colloquy of alchemists.

Harappa: If I come to you…

Asoka *(interrupting)*: No, if I'm telling you to raise demons in order to transmute slaughter, I can no way cast you in the negative. Even as you accuse me of hypocrisy in light of my murderous campaign in Kalinga you simply kindle old residue in order to bring up prior pain.

Asoka *(shaking his head)*: If . . .

Harappa *(breaking in)*: If you possessed your former self you would feed me to wolves, or evolve their listening capacity, their further capacities. Perhaps I am now floating with the dead within the mind. Perhaps I've crossed my prior form, yet it returns and powerfully commands me. *(Weary, shaking his head)* I must retire Asoka, replace me with Daro, objectify my vulnerability. Let the lynxes devour me, then allow me to walk into my open grave *(Harappa slowly disappears stage left. As he retires a cackling of ravens and crows begins to consume the stage with sound as the dimmed yellow light fades to black.)*

ACT V

AT THE DOOR OF THE LIMITLESS

SCENE I

(Daro is sitting at his work-bench carving replicas of Harappa and Asoka, carving intermittently, picking one up and putting one down. His visage reflects doubt and distraction. Quietly, the magician Pentaura enters, three-quarters visible stage left, and begins audibly whispering to him from the shadows.)

PENTAURA *(palpably whispering)*: You react too strongly to illusive charisma and sign. You seek to re-create their skeletal shadows yet you hesitate.

(Daro then fingers the handle of his carving knife, hesitant to stick it in either one of the figures.)

PENTAURA *(at a more audible level)*: As if you were master of magic, as if you resurrect corpses and escort them to Sekmet so that they live at a parallel remove. So that she can protract them the power that is killing. *(Pause)* Your eyes no longer spin, your power seems missing. You breathe as though air was caught in your nostrils.

(Pentaura then fully appears walking in ever widening circles around Daro's work-bench, arrayed in a black robe trimmed in yellow and red.)

PENTAURA *(in motion)*: You are gnawed by imbalance. *(as a prosecutor)* Their old charisma rots before you. Say, you turn Harappa into a lynx in order to slay him. Or say, you turn Asoka into a group of falcons strangely lost to themselves headed out to sea. How would you then transmute the threat that writhes inside your solar plexus? It's as if you wade in liminal nettling where numerics spread and disintegrate, where the moon falls in fire. Daro, if I sought to command you, my ire would refract from your deafness. Because of this I feel it is time to hold council with your spirit. *(Continuing to circle)* Imagine you exist as embodied umbra surreptitiously escaped from dark umbilical nets. At the cusp of visual fertilization you magically command the movement of ghostly swans floating in your blood. And these swans begin to exalt themselves as occult verticality, no longer in possession of the stationary power of your former personality. From vernacular perspective, you exist as none other than position-less surfeit, the blank identity of dust. By means of such extremes you will tend to transmute as RA blazing as its own infinite identity. This is other than transmuting as if you could transmute the soul for 100,000 years, and then begin to sense initial shifting when the universe erupted into a combinatory hail, as if one attempted by means of directed instigation to create an illuminated lantern, hanging, so that the source of vertigo creates overwhelming effect. Then the source of vertigo will erupt. Fever will cease to embrace you, yet, you will wake up depleted no longer able to govern the form of Daro as he was.

(Daro stares blankly into space. He drops his carving knife. He then turns to Pentaura who has vanished. He then picks up the knife in order to hack at the carving of Harappa. His energies quickly fail. He then lays his head on the carving table riddled by astonishment and confusion.)

SCENE II

(Khonsu, arrayed in white, with whitened face and hands suddenly appears before Asoka as an unbidden apparition. Rays of diffuse white light punctuate the dimmed yellow light of the chamber.)

ASOKA *(startled, with a slight trembling of his voice)*: You are a swarm of knives attempting to injure my shadow. *(Hesitation begins to pervade his voice)* Can you answer me Khonsu? Who ascribes the forces that kindle their waves against me? Do you empower Harappa in employing the magic of serpents against me? Do you trans-mix the fates so that I waver?

KHONSU *(with hollow voice)*: An uncertain aura exists about you. You run hot and cold, you are endangered by lapses. You must know that Daro struggles in a lower field that you've already transcended. Do you intend to lift him, to harmonize his presence so as to sway him from self-haunting? He has now carved your image from wax and is wavering at this hour waiting to see for himself if he will plunge his knife into your form. He feels he can no longer balance himself. He wavers at the door of the limitless. You exist in his mind as symbol of the absolute, as unshaken form, at times, occluded by the Sun. It seems at some level you seek to animate his doubt, to foment in his heart a fundamental uncertainty. Or do you employ him as a sigil so that he mutilates Harappa's figurine thereby casting him-self into hell.

ASOKA *(a blank look in his eyes)*: You utter something other than circumstantial harvest. *(Slowly rising)* You must know the density in my heart sends out rumour and burden. *(Now standing, slightly wavering)* I'm feeling the imminence of Psychostasia. I've passed through the storms of 100,000 years. Yet I have no need to bow down and cast myself in someone else's skin. Because I've risen above conjecture and rancour anxiousness continues to suffuse me with its antonyms. Yet I am moving towards the Sun. As for scraps of pedestals or silver I wish for none. Since I've staved off the fires of my own execution, my power is now unstated. I am no longer the God transfixed by weaponry and slaughter. I empathize with the woe of mammals, with the struggles of pierced oxen, with the woe of birds that burn with cold. These are internal havens non-condensed by coded seals. According to Harappa I am convulsed by corruption, that I am served exclusive compost by animated lions, spliced by syllables of intrigue.

KHONSU *(his hands behind his back almost floating back and forth)*: You've built a gourd of ashes and now you've drowned it. Now you speak through the unintentional. For you Asoka the Sun is a sign that exists, but yet, does not exist. It is neither visible nor invisible, it hovers as if it were scattered salt imploded by unseen stricture, you quite rightly say that nothing applies. As physical body you know the in-gargantuan as habitat, as a palace of moons listening to the rise and fall of vapour. *(Pauses motion and stands face to face with wavering Asoka)* Let Harappa and Daro come to their own sense of balance. Let them attempt to harmonize their self-defining harassment of one another. Let them cross the lightning abyss. Let them self-renounce their paralytic view.

(The diffuse white light fades in tandem with the dimmed yellow light. The stage goes dark to the sound of sistrums shaking.)

SCENE III

(Harappa keeps counsel with himself, sitting at a round wooden table hurriedly blowing a paper boat across a large bowl of water.)

HARAPPA *(muttering to himself)*: I will sail to Egypt so as to harvest silk and jade from China. Then I will bring both harvests back to Sind. The state apparatus will no longer conceal me. I, who have opened a boat of asps so that my soldiers can fully measure their own wrath. They who will toil for me under my incandescent auspices at the beck and call of my own bidding knowing that eventually Sind will be mine; I will re-punish Kalinga, never having as my plan inclination for the healing of animals. Of course not all forms are sacred. Asoka's inclination seems not to include me. My mind has never lost its power. What I know is that boats sail, battles occur, and bodies succumb from mayhem. In order to provoke such power I command in myself aphoristic ravens, a phalanx of vipers, and archers who ride lynxes.

(A flash of light breaks through the dimness. Harappa seems startled. He stands up slightly turning his head from side to side as if expecting some form to appear. After several tense moments he begins to settle into his chair continuing to blow the paper boat across the bowl, periodically looking up and down for forms to appear, all the while projecting a curiously shaken posture. The stage darkens.)

SCENE IV

(Beneath the dim yellow, Khonsu appears moving from the darkness of stage left into view. He remains arrayed in whiteness, his face painted white, initially accompanied by the sound of gongs.)

KHONSU *(lowered tone)*: You need call them together Asoka, not in terms of a well of water, but drawing them both to the well of loyalty. They both waver. You will gather them together in an optimum dimension. As you must know, I am not speaking of law, or provoking repetitive confrontation. You are simply building blazes from calmness. Daro pervades one side of eclipse, Harappa another. It is simply your fate to balance the powers of sand. When each of them bellows, you must calm your own interior inferno, your own courageousness of habit.

ASOKA *(offstage)*: Their threads of blood shift as opposite tonalities. Perhaps I can hone them to such a degree that they can never lapse into quandary.

KHONSU: I'll summon them. *(Right arm pointing upwards)* Return to the Sun for a quarter of a fortnight.

(Darkness suddenly engulfs the stage all the while there are voices off stage humming in tune with barely perceptible gongs. Harappa and Daro appear from opposite sides of the stage warily moving towards one another. The dimmed yellow light mingles with a diffuse white light. There is a brushing of symbols mixed with bells and fleeting notes from a bass clarinet. The two avery their eyes from one another as they move closer and closer to one another. The sound stops. Complete tension grips the atmosphere. Asoka slowly descends from the rafters on an ornate wooden scaffold flanked by small carved lion's heads. When reaching the stage he steps off the scaffold with a bright blue urn filled with feathers in

his left hand and places it midway between both Ministers like an axial point between two opposing forces, the scaffold is deftly covered by black curtains imprinted with lions's heads.)

ASOKA *(arms outstretched)*: All former actions have been dissolved and now proclaim themselves as dust. *(He slowly retracts his arms.)*

HARAPPA *(suspicious tone)*: I remain the dazed animal whose actions are dust. *(looking askance at Daro)* So now we consume living as old contorted skin.

(Daro now stands apart remaining wary of the both of them.)

HARAPPA *(definitively speaking to Asoka)*: I remain your First Minister.

ASOKA: Does this mean that you have ascended your own fever?

HARAPPA: I feel plummeted, cast into inferior realms in spite of my bravery.

DARO: He is not attacking you Harappa. You…

HARAPPA *(confronting Daro)*: I've not chosen argument.

DARO: I'm speaking of height and air that engenders no Imperial registration.

HARAPPA: So now you both contest me.

ASOKA: Have either one of you experienced the spontaneous field that swallows the abyss?

HARAPPA: We are not blind followers, or caricatures of false summation.

ASOKA *(holding in anger)*: Harappa one needs ascend above toil. *(Pointing to Daro)* I need you to tend the incalculable through husbandry.

DARO *(incredulous)*: So we are reduced to slaves, to the maintenance of ziggurats?

ASOKA *(partially commanding)*: Daro you will mend soils and bring the territory to health. Harappa, you will carve scriptures into rock. *(A slight pause)* I know I've stirred up frightening waves and conjured monstrous principates. I know you have both eaten flame and cut pressure with swords. To you both, it seems I do nothing other than imbue illusive ancillary drift. I now ask that you both provide effort in chronicling sheaves. This is not skill that conjoins with the principles of hardened command.

DARO: You throttle us with philosophical commotion.

HARAPPA: You no longer command our movement through rivers of blood.

ASOKA: No judgement commands you! *(After protracted silence, he is suddenly bathed in a shaft of blue light, speaking as if possessed)* As if I appeared through apsidal orbits while striding through frustrums. Yet I need not baffle the both of you with rudiments, with the basic equation of your destiny. *(Pointing to the urn)* Think of this urn as having feathers of khesau grass. Think of them as flying inside of themselves as vanishment being invisible moons in transition. Therefore I ascribe to night the day, and day to night as we evolve inside this chronic nether light. Thus, the Sun is a median spinning, is an occulted diorite.

HARAPPA: Your thoughts stammer.

ASOKA (*looking warily in all directions*): The shadows continue to spin.

HARAPPA: You've told me without any notion of surcease that fiends continue to populate my blood.

DARO (*focusing on Harappa*): You house channa in your skull. You re-ingest the flames from its menace.

HARAPPA (*accusatory*): You enable him Daro.

ASOKA: You both need rise above prior slaughter. I have no need to wrap your souls in black hair, or pierce your sides with daggers in order to release smoke. I have not regarded both of you as being shadowed by the Hemhem crown, or by Haubna-aru-her-hra keeping away rains and storms. I am parallel to Seker, God of the occulted Sun. I, who open day as magic by force of the buried Sun. And being the buried Sun I float from occulted seaports in heaven this being indelible calisthenics, my higher proof, my depth of fate.

HARAPPA: So you announce our age as fire, as being the ruined Sun come to life out of ashes.

DARO (*slightly trembling*): My balance feels lost, my bones feel as though they're bleeding.

ASOKA (*calmly*): It means the higher forces are stirring in your system.

HARAPPA (*looking at both Asoka and Daro, quivering with anger*): What levels are you planning, shifting ice to summer, making lynxes calmly sprawl atop your tables?

DARO: Your suspicion is groundless Harappa.

HARAPPA *(derisively)*: You silently shift the burden to Asoka in order to make me relent so that I cease to chisel rock by my breathing.

ASOKA *(turning to Harappa)*: Daylight brings health, nature's forces are multiplied by its facility.

DARO *(more composed, addressing Harappa)*: You're leaking embitterment, the clauses you foment are broken.

HARAPPA: So you deny in this roundabout manner your wish for my demise. My approaching skeletal dust seems to befit you.

ASOKA *(again focusing upon Harappa)*: My blood calls out to you. The path you've chosen has been condemned.

HARAPPA *(bitterly)*: So now I am Minister as enemy, and you as Seker, as Priya-darshi, as "Beloved of the Gods," single me out for mortal injury.

ASOKA: You're presaging your own memorial. Storms of inner cinder have disrupted your orientation. Your extremity seems no longer warranted.

HARAPPA *(angrily shifts towards Asoka)*: You tell me I am blind!

(Harappa reaches for his dagger, Daro intercedes, they grapple. The lion curtain opens and Asoka ascends part way on the scaffold. He begins pointing his index finger at both of them, and the conflict begins to ease. Then without warning Harappa reaches for his fallen dagger, and again Daro drags him down. Asoka raises his palms upward and the Three Magicians suddenly swarm amulets across the stage while chanting.)

IN UNISON: An owl has formed
               And struggles for resurrection
               An owl has formed
               And struggles for resurrection

(Asoka descends to the stage on the scaffold, the lion curtains part so that the is scaffold is hidden. Asoka steps forward, the magicians withdraw.)

ASOKA *(staring at the fallen ministers)*: You self-feast upon yourselves as if you were a scattering of worms. Your powers have now fallen, you stamp your marks upon the abyss.

DARO *(looking up at Asoka incredulous)*: I have sought to save you and now you only restore wrath.

(The two ministers disentangle themselves and slowly gain standing positions, standing parallel to one another so that the three of them form a triangular position with Asoka standing about a half dozen steps in front of them.)

ASOKA *(commanding tone)*: I need both of you to mend yourselves, to refuse suffocation and panic. Wait, bide time, let Osiris and Durga balance in your veins. *(Focusing upon Harappa)* If you were a fiend, or an immoral lizard, would I have lifted you to levels that balance life and death? *(Focusing on Daro)* Would I ask the same of you?

(Daro and Harappa shift their gaze downward and then slowly raise their heads collectively.)

HARAPPA *(seeming to struggle, almost squinting)*: So you ask me to bury my own instinct and scribble moral toxin on stone. *(Pointing to himself)* I am more aligned to Nanda and his policy. I exterminate Kshatriya's as I sleep.

ASOKA *(walking in a semi-circle hands behind his back)*: You complicate matters Harappa, you form your own misnomer.

DARO *(suddenly cutting in, pointing at Harappa)*: He only considers fire and its embittered immobility!

HARAPPA: So if I continue to ride lions into battle I remain nothing more than a burdensome chimera…

DARO *(intensely)*: Douse the imperial chariots!

HARAPPA: You continue to require of me the opposite of myself.

ASOKA: If I sought to renew the purity of old tensions how would the immeasurable begin to breathe. I know that all the soldiers will breathe through the teeth of revelation pledged to empty the coffers for the doing of good. No, I have not unleashed mirages simply to expose my own uncertainty. Harappa, how can I now kill if I've razed its possibility?

HARAPPA *(loudly defending himself)*: So you render me crude and powerless.

DARO *(focusing on Harappa)*: You reduce all larger motion, you square the palpable with false solution!

HARAPPA *(breaking in)*: You falsely execute stricture.

HARAPPA: How can I falsely execute stricture when everything you say drives me towards the hive of mutilation, to mothers riddled with wounds?

DARO: You make your own wheel and ruthlessly spin it.

HARAPPA *(begins pulling off his protective armour)*: Then flay me and spill my blood for the dogs.

ASOKA *(calmly)*: You wish for violent fulfillment as the lone charioteer charging into arrows.

HARAPPA: So how can bravery be treason?

ASOKA: The state has transmuted. All of my actions now proselytize the invisible; panic as cadence has now dissolved, hectic instigation no longer applies.

DARO: The infallible?

ASOKA: That which ceases to fall from the horizon, that which elicits the hidden.

DARO: Is our potion to be brewed by obscurity?

ASOKA: All the time I ask myself, will such potion ever be understood? Will its dimensions ever balance? Will its doubt be ever broached?

HARAPPA *(in a searching manner)*: It seems you do nothing but repeat and replenish yourself by repeating.

ASOKA: So if you open up a cave of demons and applaud your own agony...

HARAPPA: I am nothing more than chimerical exhibit. You seem to simplify all struggle.

ASOKA: As you speak Harappa, mirrors burn, forces destroy their own powers.

HARAPPA: I feel you've cast me as a ghost whose hair has turned cold and kindled pox on the wheat.

ASOKA *(glancing at Daro)*: Harappa, if you sift part of the part and continue parting a part of that part, you can never know the part of the part you are seeking. Thus, there is activity by blindness, by cartographical chaos, which forces you to itemize spent kindling according to self-constructed mathematics.

HARAPPA *(shifting back and forth in one place)*: Again you renounce me to the announcement of old form. *(Pause)* If I am so shadowed by such fatigue why does not Sind now wallow in damage? *(Loudly)* I've earned the tensions that I carry.

DARO *(under his breath)*: You've done nothing more than cross a blizzard of thorns, nothing other than…

HARAPPA *(his head snapping towards Daro)*: I fear no scorn from the dead. I continue to judge and execute dilemma. I am the one who has power over phrasing.

ASOKA: Stop retreating in yourself. You tend to pester your own fate.

HARAPPA: Asoka, let me chisel my own walls.

DARO: Asoka is speaking of new medicine in the blood. Your scorched abrasives…

ASOKA: You brood like an insolvent hunter…

DARO: Speak to others Harappa. There are many nameless in the countryside that no longer obscure compassion, nor take up disruption as a mode of belief.

HARAPPA: So if I fail to kill on the royal hunt it seems I would beckon self-erosion and foment strategic ailment.

ASOKA: You're prodding for a concrete counter-position.

HARAPPA: You've shadowed my body with multiple animosity…

(Suddenly Asoka waves his arms and red streaks flash across the stage and vanish. Harappa looks skyward and struggles to maintain his balance.)

DARO *(sarcastically)*: He knows that the Sun is other than carved rock.

(Harappa remains silent. Asoka remains stock-still. Daro, feeling somehow renewed feels power surging through his viscera.)

DARO: Asoka needs no stones to verbalize ruins, nor does he author a tenuous half-moon to command general destiny.

HARAPPA *(annoyed)*: You are blatant Daro. So if I ask you to vocalize and send rain, or make ravens loom larger, can you provide me with example?

DARO: I'm simply resuming my quest for other capabilities of strength.

HARAPPA: You tell me your thoughts sustain no evil,that you've crossed the threshold of paradise, all the while you threaten by obliqueness. *(Loudly, circling Daro again)* War has ceased to tame me!

DARO: You thrive on pain and you judge others by that pain. *(pointing to Asoka)* He rules by astonishment, by measures which seem to flare from the obscure. He rules by spontaneous abdication, always opening paths by inscrutable vapour. *(Turning to Harappa)* You continue to pursue predation, you are plunged in hierarchical seizure.

HARAPPA *(starring at Asoka and Daro)*: You crawl the continent of skin like arachnids attempting to soak my derma in venom. One of you hides and comes forth from their hiding seemingly humbled by nuance. It's the intrigue that sickens me, which leaves everything gainless. It's diplomacy by stealth, by infernal leakage, which links itself to perjury, to utterance by false measure. *(Extending his chest and circling them)* Imagine me as your leader, with all my decrees emitted by nervous beckoning. As an Emperor who gorges himself on idolatry, who mixes fact with prevarication, riding his chariot of diamonds across a falsely sculpted rock bed. My eyes then rendered as iconic wood relief, always leering with rage, my torso entangled by summary mis-alignment. *(Asoka and Daro remaining silent but enraged)* I would race to the Sun simply to cause havoc, with my voice unable to tremble, or exert its concern for non-incendiary training. I would darken the tops of mountains so that dawn would never reflect itself. Upon occasion I would be imbued by interregnums so that power would concur through doubt, having shadows merge with crumbling solstice mirrors. *(Now focusing on Asoka)* By governing from suspension I would have my remains soaked by fire, by smoke engulfed elephants of war, all my efforts always parallel to annihilation.

ASOKA *(quietly gaining composure)*: Harappa I acknowledge Kalinga. I acknowledge King Kharabela. The war elephants, yes, the Daya River red with blood, the throats slashed, the permanately scorched by blindness, the sorrow brought to bear and denied. Call me prone to Ahmisa, to Dhamma, it is my understanding that the Buddha fled Egypt under the throes of the Cambyses, and now he quells my desire for parching and upheaval, for the need of one person to willfully destroy the lives of others. At this level of my odyssey I feel suspended above a ravine of beasts always at odds with my own adjustment. I've lost my impulse to slay, to engorge prisoners with their own suffering, only to create from these actions hypocritical restitution. You ask me about the law of invariable framing, of my justice that declares itself according to corpses. You ask me of the purpose that issues

104

from palpable power. There exists no action or result confirmed by boundary. You suggest that I've now wandered into scattered leakage as rule. Yes, I've raided innocent marrow in error, I've shredded prone bodies, so how can such action render balance, or aggrandize itself according to principles of malice? *(Continuing to stare at Harappa)* You come to me with foils and needles, with dilemmas exuding from your eyes which seem to corrupt on contact. You accuse me of promoting hesitation and distance. You want to cultivate blindness at the cusp of revelation wanting me to sail across purposeless oceans and vanish. This is…

HARAPPA *(breaking in)*: Master, if I burden your solar chromicity, or contort your seminal scale of equation, it is because I've absorbed hostility, and broken bread in its desert.

ASOKA *(raising his voice slightly)*: The horizon remains unwrought. It is not a stalk of wheat that bends at dawn by the wind. It never spirals as displacement. *(Walking back and forth like a lawyer explaining his case)* I thought at a former that I was the superior raptor, that I was the one blinding symbol risen above language. This was nothing other than frenzy Harappa. Because of this I settled upon law by blood, by its seepage from disorder. Wonder for me was none other than an incinerated field.

HARAPPA *(sarcastic)*: So you poetically claim your own personal justice so as to reach the Sun with your name. You mis-state your own courageousness.

DARO: If anything Harappa, you inflame all the wounds of past effort, so that we are limited by the ill-begotten. To you, every speech is criminal by deception.

ASOKA *(having stopped starts pacing again)*: Understand Harappa, it is only the superficial plane that darkens and corrodes our thinking. It carries a terseness about it, it fogs speech with riddles through particulates.

HARAPPA *(more openly defiant)*: You use wisdom to impugn me, to leak your private skill so that it remains just beyond the accepted limits.

DARO *(sharply to Harappa)*: You extol a maimed system!

HARAPPA *(heatedly)*: If I waken old error I waken old error.

DARO: You threaten me with unstinting liquidation. *(Turning to Asoka)* Must we continue to exercise our thought upon prior ruination, upon open graves and their odour?

HARAPPA: Have I ever justified gratuitous murder, or sought its enactment via surreptitious incursion? If I lie about this I regale Asoka for just punishment. I have no need to prevaricate just to in-state my own magnificence.

DARO: It seems with every breath you pursue your own harassment.

ASOKA *(to both parties)*: The atmosphere is absorbed with vestiges of violence. There is constant loss from in-justice, by a morale fate that corrupts its own unleashing. I know I have been convinced by error, by ruination that has flooded my pores. If I counsel escape to the nameless, omniscience revolves and understands its own paradox by absence. Therefore I am not the old Asoka, I have risen above my former edicts in order that my throne will be cleansed by vibration. I am now rider-less, released by my own in-possession. *(Focusing on Harappa)* You waste yourself by focus upon affliction. *(Quickly turning to Daro)* You need open yourself to realms that free you from doubt. *(Re-focusing upon Harappa)* I need you to return to the field and gather the wounded bodies, then speak to yourself and absorb spontaneous power from the forests. Anoint invisibility, have the soldiers build housing, and cast your darkness to the un-returnable. Remember, it is not personal need that I seek to inscribe upon columns, but merely to summarize the un-scalable. This being power by transcendental stellar current never bound by outer law.

(Voices begin to enunciate off stage in a melodious drone)

CHORUS: The origin of balance is indestructible

It is electrical flow

It is the zodiac subtended by non-conflicted aura

It is purity of our enriched planetary axis

It is gain conducted through the spiral of life

It is the compound levels open to self-witness

It is threaded by potential as Nirvana

ASOKA *(gazing vertically)*: Harappa, you will sleep in black water and rise as a scroll from osmosis. You will allow yourself enrichment by elemental spell, you will rise as enveloped enigma.

(Asoka then imperceptibly shifts backwards through the partially opened lion curtain and begins ascending on the wooden scaffold, as the dimmed light gradually darkens, as Harappa and Daro slowly ambulate about one another in stunned movement. Flutes, bells, and voices begin to intermingle, casting an aural spell. Then a series of soldiers quietly enter the stage from all directions spontaneously unarming themselves scattering their daggers into a pile, as the stage darkens to the sound of string bass and the ringing of bells.)

About the Author

In the tradition of Sun Ra and Aime Cesaire, Will Alexander's poetry combines the surreal with an extra-terrestrial perspective on the relation of humans to mind and the cosmic environment. His perspective emerges from Africa and the Earth's trans-oceanic rim. He is also a poet, essayist, novelis, philosopher, visual artist, as well as playwright. His myriad books include *Vertical Rainbow Climber* (1987), *Asia & Haiti* (1995), A*bove the Human Nerve Domain* (1998), *Towards the Primeval Lightning Field* (1999), *Exobiology as Goddess* (2004), *Sunrise Armageddon* (2006), and *The Sri Lankan Loxodrome* (2009). A Whiting Fellow, a PEN Oakland National Book Award recipient, and the winner of the Jackson Poetry Prize for 2016. Will Alexander lives and works in Los Angeles.

About CHAX

Founded in 1984 in Tucson, Arizona, Chax has published 200 books in a variety of formats, including hand printed letterpress books and chapbooks, hybrid chapbooks, book arts editions, and trade paperback editions such as the book you are holding. In August 2014 Chax moved to Victoria, Texas, and is presently located in the University of Houston-Victoria Center for the Arts, which has generously supported the publication of *At Night on the Sun*, which has also received support from many friends of the press. Chax is an independent 501(c)(3) organization which depends on support from various government and private funders, and, primarily, from individual donors and readers.

Recent and current books-in-progress include *The Complete Light Poems*, by Jackson Mac Low, *Life–list*, by Jessica Smith, *Andalusia*, by Susan Thackrey, *Diesel Hand*, by Nico Vassilakis, *Dark Ladies*, by Steve McCaffery, *What We Do*, by Michael Gottlieb, *Limerence*, by Saba Razvi, *Short Course*, by Ted Greenwald and Charles Bernstein, *An Intermittent Music*, by Ted Pearson, *Arrive on Wave*, by Gil Ott, *Entangled Bank*, by James Sherry, *Autocinema*, by Gaspar Orozco, *The Letters of Carla, the letter b.*, by Benjamin Hollander, *A Mere Ica*, by Linh Dinh, and *Visible Instruments*, by Michael Kelleher.

You may find CHAX online at http://chax.org